COUNTRY LIVING

Country Gardening

COUNTRY LIVING

Country Gardening

Classic Flowers
Modern Techniques
Timeless Beauty

Niña Williams &
Rebecca R. Sawyer

HEARST BOOKS
A Division of Sterling Publishing Co., Inc.
NEW YORK

This book was previously published under the title
Country Living Country Gardens.

Produced by Smallwood & Stewart, Inc., New York City
Editor Rachel Carley
Designer: Dirk Kaufman
Illustrator Willie Sunga

Library of Congress Cataloging-in-Publication Data
Available upon request.

10 9 8 7 6 5 4 3 2 1

First paperback edition 2003
Published by Hearst Books
A Division of Sterling Publishing Company, Inc.
387 Park Avenue South, New York, N.Y. 10016

www.countryliving.com

Distributed in Canada by Sterling Publishing
c/o Canadian Manda Group, One Atlantic Avenue, Suite 105
Toronto, Ontario, Canada M6K 3E7

Distributed in Australia by Capricorn Link (Australia) Pty. Ltd.
P.O. Box 704, Windsor, NSW 2756 Australia

Manufactured in China

ISBN 1-58816-320-2

IRELAND
levington
MOSS PEAT
MOSS PEAT

chapter four

House & Garden

113

chapter five

Garden Furnishings

153

chapter six

Plant List and Bibliography

193

Foreword

My introduction to the world of gardening came ~ as it did for many of my generation ~ during the Second World War, when we were encouraged to do our part for the war effort by planting "Victory Gardens." The neighborhood divided some unused property adjacent to the school grounds into square plots and set about planting vegetables.

I still remember with fondness how my parents became increasingly involved in this rewarding hobby. Each year their crops grew more abundant as their knowledge and expertise broadened. It was during this period that I learned that if you buried a piece of potato with an eye in it, a plant would magically appear to produce a full-size potato in the fall. One year, my father, whose job it was to dig up the potatoes, missed one. The following autumn he found the missed spud grown to the size of a small boulder; we had mashed potatoes for a week from that prize!

By the end of the war, when my parents transferred their efforts to their own yard, they had become impassioned gardeners. The vegetable patch had been transformed to a flower garden. My mother, who had never been a club woman, joined the local garden club ~ eventually becoming its president. For the rest of her life she spent most of her free time filling our yard with every imaginable flowering plant, bush, and tree. My father, an artist and sculptor, took an interest in fruit-bearing trees, and experimented for years with different types of apple trees; when his experiments didn't work, the trunks were recycled into sculptures.

Since the apple doesn't fall far from the tree, I tried my own hand at gardening. My busy schedule doesn't leave me the time for the full-blown English-style garden I would love to have, but when I had a home in the country I took great pride in a wildflower garden I planted. In my present apartment in the center of Manhattan I'm fortunate to have wonderfully wide windowsills and lots of light. So, since I wouldn't think of living without plants, I tend several ongoing indoor projects, including a living ivy wreath and a four-foot Norfolk pine that I started as a seedling in a terrarium.

Alas, most of my gardening these days is limited to dreaming . . . but thankfully that is not the case with the two passionate gardeners on our staff, Niña Williams and Rebecca Sawyer. We hope that this book, a true labor of love about their labor of love, will bring you many happy hours in your garden. And if, like me, you can only dream, dream along with me.

Rachel Newman
Editor Emerita, *Country Living*

Introduction

On our editorial travels for *Country Living*, we have often noticed that people welcome us warmly not only into their homes but that they also especially enjoy ushering us into their gardens. Whether these dedicated gardeners are nurturing a patch of vegetables or sowing a field of wildflowers, it is clear that their colorful and inviting plots reflect the same heartfelt pride of place that distinguishes their houses.

Indeed, over the last decade the enthusiasm for country gardening has steadily intensified. In keeping with the hospitable spirit of American country ways, we continuously meet new friends who are eager to share their ideas and know-how. During photography sessions, our hosts often refresh us with minted ice tea and lemonade, sustain us with herb-strewn salads at lunch, and delight us with exuberant bouquets ~ all bounty gathered from gardens just a few steps away. Many, too, hand over cuttings and valuable bits of advice as we exchange farewells, and stay in touch to let us know how their gardens are evolving.

These encounters make us ever more aware of how much a garden, no matter how small or simple, enhances the quality of life. Nowhere is this more true than in a country garden, which, by definition, is the essence of informality, ease, and individual expression. In the country garden, there is not only a willingness to mix plants and to experiment, but also the real desire to respect a given site, and to enhance it with plantings that will feel at home there.

The country garden is also likely to reflect a distinct regard for history. Witness the recent interest in heirloom gardening, a movement to reintroduce and preserve flowers, fruits, and vegetables lost or forgotten when they were made obsolete by new tastes and modern hybrids. In the same vein, there is a renewed demand for vigorous old-fashioned roses. Their lush look and rich fragrance epitomize the nostalgia that permeates many country gardens.

While country gardens have much in common, they also display an enormous diversity, embracing tiny dooryards, city rooftops, suburban tracts, expansive farmsteads, and woodlands alike. We invite you to visit some of the many we have enjoyed, and to share the personal experiences and accomplishments of our readers. What other pastime than gardening could better capture the imagination and hearts of those who love "country"?

Niña Williams and Rebecca Sawyer

chapter one

AMERICAN COUNTRY GARDENS

As the imaginative approaches and rich variety of designs illustrated in this chapter prove, country gardens find a place in all regions of the country. Indeed, adaptable and free-spirited, they can take virtually any form, depending on the dictates of climate and location. Be it a Manhattan entryway softened with climbing vines, a New England cutting border, a Texas rose garden, or a field of Colorado poppies, a garden is "country" as long as the look is natural and the mood welcoming.

While some plants instantly evoke a strong sense of place ~ as cacti suggest the desert terrain of the Southwest, for example ~ others defy regional classification, growing equally well from East Coast to West. Yet, while they are decidedly individual, all the gardens shown here go beyond the ordinary, expressing both the joy and the satisfaction experienced by those who have planted and tended them. Never quite "done," they serve as inspiration to all country gardeners ~ with or without green thumbs.

Set off by a box hedge and picket fence, golden trumpet narcissi make a simple but cheerful roadside garden on Massachusetts' Nantucket Island (opposite). Preferring slightly sandy soil, these springtime favorites thrive near the seaside, growing best in full sun or light shade. Climbing roses, which also do well in a damp climate, frame a Nantucket window (above) for a classic country look. Winter-hardy ramblers such as the single-petaled 'American Pillar' feature flexible canes that are easily trained up the sides of buildings.

A tubful of easy-to-grow annuals, including zinnias, cleomes, and sunflowers, symbolizes the carefree informality of a Long Island, New York, cutting garden (above). Blooms like these will lend exuberant color all summer long indoors and out. Also located in New York State, a lush poolside perennial garden (opposite) has completely transformed a former parking area. Roses, irises, daisies, sundrops, and yarrow in staggered heights follow the undulating edge of the pool while creating a lawn border distinguished by texture and depth.

A small entry garden in New York City (left) is enlivened by potted geraniums, a vigorous wisteria, and climbing roses. Rather than pruning the rose bush into obedience, the owners have allowed it to grow in a relaxed fashion. A small vineyard makes an unusual backyard garden for a stone farmhouse in the Delaware River Valley (opposite). Situated on a southern slope, the plants benefit from ample sunshine, while a mature shade tree cools the house.

Mauve phlox supplies a mass of color to the front yard of a former stagecoach stop and hotel in Ohio (above). Old-fashioned perennials such as these are happy choices for historic properties, as they help re-create the ambience of an earlier time. The peeled-log fence reinforces an unfussy appearance; variegated snow-on-the-mountain forms a thick ground cover at its base. In West Virginia (right), mature trees and an informal yard rimmed by a split-rail fence enhance the atmosphere of rural simplicity.

Featuring parallel beds lined by dirt paths, the perennial garden displays classic Shasta daisies and lamb's ears, joined by more unusual spikelike kniphofia, or torch lily, a plant native to Africa. In a corral-side garden (overleaf), a dramatic burst of blooms illustrates the visual power of Oriental poppies. These brilliantly hued flowers, which flourish at high altitudes, have adapted well to their Colorado site. Clover adds purple accents.

Country gardens often showcase a mix of flowers and vegetables. In the homey backyard plot of a Minnesota log house (above), sun-loving zinnias and tomatoes promise a visual as well as culinary feast. Completely different in scale, a vast field of dandelions (right) provides a stunning foreground for an open Colorado vista ~ and proves that one person's weed is another's wildflower. The curving drive and layers of shrubs and trees break up the view in a pleasing way, and gradually draw the eye to the mountain backdrop.

Although hybridizing techniques have created the near-perfect synthesis of color and form seen in the modern tea rose, country gardeners often prefer the blowsy demeanor and heady scent of old-fashioned varieties. 'Old Blush,' the star of a Texas garden (left), is a China rose that first made its way west from the Orient in 1733. This variety produces not only sumptuous blossoms, but also decorative hips in autumn. Nearby on the same property, 'Zéphirine Drouhin,' a nearly thornless pink Bourbon (above), flourishes in the Southern sun, captivating passersby with its intense perfume.

ROOMS & MEALS
TOURISTS WELCOME

Outside an adobe-style house in New Mexico (opposite), pots of chrysanthemums which can be moved to sun or shade, as weather dictates, surround a half barrel of drought-tolerant petunias. An Arizona garden (above) features cacti in a variety of shapes and sizes, including prickly pear, barrel, and cholla (or teddy bear) cactus. The colors of the blossoms look particularly rich against desert soil.

Red valerian enhances a rambling border garden (above) contained by a white picket fence. The look is reminiscent of an East Coast cottage garden; in fact, California is the setting. An equally informal atmosphere was created in a charming Oregon yard (opposite), where masses of foxgloves, statice, bachelor's buttons, daisies, and rudbeckias bloom in free-spirited profusion.

Lacking traditional front yards, houseboat residents off Sausalito, California, rely on containers to create a riot of color (above). This fragrant seaside garden includes potted Burmese honeysuckle, bougainvillea, orchids, jasmine, phlox, and herbs. A dreamy wisteria-draped building near Santa Barbara, California, nestles in a cottage garden (right) where plants overflow in characteristic abundance. A hedge of glossy-leaved camellias and stately blue-flowered agapanthus, a member of the amaryllis family, line the walk. Both flowering plants are well suited to a temperate climate.

chapter two

OUR FAVORITE GARDENS

Over the years, *Country Living* has had the pleasure of visiting some of the most appealing country gardens in America. On the following pages we present five of our favorites. Displaying the special interests of their particular owners, each of these remarkable landscapes has its own story to tell.

One, for example, illustrates how careful, comprehensive planning and a clever mixture of perennials and annuals transformed a former horse pasture into a garden that looks as though it had been in place for generations. Quite different in feeling, a spare seaside landscape stands as fulfillment of another gardener's desire to showcase indigenous grasses and flowers. In yet a third version, a small yard illustrates how two resourceful homeowners created country charm in an urban setting by designing a classic cottage garden reminiscent of those found throughout the English countryside. Pure fantasy was the inspiration for another couple's delightful "hobby" garden, which, planted to scale, was designed to show off their collection of miniature trains. And finally, we take you to a cut-flower farm owned by a family who decided to turn their love of gardening into a full-time business enterprise.

An Established Garden

Colorful perennial borders radiant from seasons of pampering, vegetable patches that know no bounds, rose beds in extravagant bloom: The look is timeless, and it takes years to cultivate.

Or does it? Astute gardeners follow certain guidelines to achieve an established feeling in a surprisingly short time period. They work with masses of the same species instead of mixing lots of individual plants in one place; they use quick-growing annuals to fill out immature perennial beds; and they choose garden structures, furnishings, containers, and ornaments made of natural, indigenous materials.

If this Oregon garden is any measure, the guidelines work. In just two years, the 30-by-120-foot plot was transformed from an untended horse pasture into a handsome composition of flower, vegetable, and herb beds, all contained by tidy edgings and unified by a network of gravel pathways. Inspired by a visit to George Washington's gardens at Mount Vernon in Virginia, the owners favored a well-ordered design - but also one with a relaxed twist. "We wanted it to be like a very proper lady whose hair keeps tumbling out from under her hat," they explain.

To make that idea a reality, the couple relied on

Annuals, perennials, herbs, and vegetables thrive in a lush Oregon garden (opposite). In the foreground, golden coreopsis and orange marigolds are clustered next to butternut squash vines for a colorful effect. To protect overflowing plants from the lawn mower, gravel was chosen for the paths instead of grass; pine timbers (left untreated when used near edibles) make tidy edgings. Statice and zucchini share a place in the sun beside a weathered chair (above left). A bench (above right) holds tools of the trade: watering can, thorn-proof gloves, dibble, and trowel.

In a vine-shaded arbor (opposite), seedlings are transplanted, plans made for the coming season, and friendly gatherings held. Pots and baskets of annuals – including giant zinnias, marigolds, lobelia, and geraniums – bring extra brightness and vigor to the still-young garden. A vintage painted-tin basket (right) displays golden-yellow zucchini blossoms, gourds, dahlias, and carrots. A fiery red gerbera awaits transplanting.

careful planning. Having little previous gardening experience, they started by using graph paper to plot out 18 geometric beds that would break up the flat terrain. Then, moving outdoors, they delineated the plots with pine two-by-fours, adjusting the original plan to accommodate the vagaries of the site and take advantage of views.

Once the beds were set, hard work was in order. Preparing the soil properly required double digging to a depth of about 1½ feet. This laborious hand-tilling process involved shoveling the soil out to the depth of a spade, loosening the subsoil with a fork, then working in sand and peat to improve drainage; well-rotted manure was also added for nutrients. As the tilling progressed, countless rocks were removed and saved for a new creek bed elsewhere on the property.

Next came the plantings, chosen specifically to create a well-settled look. Hedges of santolina, in both silver and green, flourished immediately in the mild coastal climate, as did lavender and germander. Also quick to take hold were daylilies and rubrum lilies, both dependable first-year bloomers. A reliable perennial, silvery lamb's ears proved ideal for filling in borders.

By the second year, more perennials, including campanula (planted as four-inch seedlings the previous spring), lady's mantle, baby's breath, and hardy geraniums such as the 'A.T. Johnson' variety were ready to burst forth in full glory. Annuals, including nicotianas,

A "gardening" angel (above) stands watch over the entrance to the tool shed (left), a converted pumphouse painted to look gently aged. Astilbes, veronicas, lupines, and artemisias surround the sturdy peeled-pole fence. Each year, more easy-care perennials are added to enhance the established look.

blue salvias, lobelias, cosmos, and ageratums, were used to fill out the beds, supplying extra color and "covering a multitude of sins," as the owners put it. Equally important contributors to the established look are the many roses - especially the hardy older varieties - that have mixed well with other plants. A recurrent-blooming, deep-magenta hybrid rugosa, 'Hansa,' for example, looks wonderful surrounded by drifts of pale purple lavender.

With the planting done, one of the biggest challenges was integrating a cement-block pumphouse that made an uninspired landmark at one end of the garden. Cultivating a veil of clinging ivy was an obvious approach, but camouflage was clearly required until the ivy could take hold. The immediate solution was a simple but decorative paint treatment in which a base coat of latex exterior house paint in a shade of dusty rose was applied, rubbed with a thin layer of white, then sponged with black. In this manner, it took little more than a day for the pumphouse to gain the look of weathered terra-cotta.

The ambitious garden scheme wasn't complete, however, without yet another structure: an octagonal grape arbor that has become a favorite spot for morning coffee and afternoon reflection. Built by the owners themselves, the arbor was designed with a simple framework of eight 14-foot pine posts set into holes dug 3½ feet deep. After these side posts were inserted in the ground, each hole was filled in with fine gravel, then mounded over with dirt prepared for planting.

Softening the rustic look of the arbor, Niagara grapevines meander over the roof and provide a welcome shade canopy in exchange for scant effort. "Niagara is a green seedless variety that is the perfect grape for Oregon's temperate climate," explain the owners, who prune the vines back to the fifth bud every year in early February. The results are more than gratifying. "In warm weather," they say, "we spend a good deal of time in the arbor - it's the coolest place on the property. We do most of our potting there, too."

BORDER LINES

Used thoughtfully, attractive edgings make an important contribution to a garden. As design elements, they can create eye-catching patterns, define the perimeters of beds and paths, and produce an overall effect of tidiness. They are also functional, helping to prevent weeds and grass from invading planting areas. An edging dividing a flower bed from the lawn can protect overflowing plants by keeping the mower at a distance; this also obviates the need for hand-trimming any grass that is adjacent to the bed.

A broad range of materials is suitable for edgings, and the choice often comes down to personal preference. Among the possibilities are flagstones, bricks (overlapped on an angle, or placed end to end), railroad ties, and terra-cotta curbing tiles. All of these may be set in a bed of sand for stability. Commercially made metal and plastic strips, sold at garden centers, are also available; these are flexible and work especially well for following curving contours.

Whatever the choice, it is a good idea to consider how a particular material will look with your plantings. Combinations - brick and wood, for instance - can be especially effective, providing a pleasing framework for the garden.

Spare & Simple

After years of recording other people's property on film, the New York photographer who built this seashore home decided it was time to have a place for himself. "I wanted to create my dream house," he recalls, "and I knew exactly what it would be: a simple yet classic structure that would blend with the landscape, rather than fight for attention."

For help in planning a new house that would work well on the flat, two-acre site in a former Long Island potato field, the owner turned to his cousin, an architect known for designs that respect their surroundings. Together, they opted for the clean lines of a vernacular Long Island farmhouse.

"It achieves our two principal goals," says the architect of the overall plan. "The house had to be small - less than 2,000 square feet in area - and, with neighbors so close, there had to be privacy." To get it, he placed a detached garage on one side of the backyard and a wisteria-covered pergola on the other, effectively enclosing the space to create an outdoor "room."

Tying the house and yard to the surrounding landscape, a mix of hybrid perennials and grasses furthers the success of the design. Near the house, tall, indigenous grasses were left in place, as were many other native seashore plants. To enhance the natural effect, a meadow of wildflowers suited to the northeastern climate was sown on the street-side border of the property and filled out with seedling perennials. The result: a spare landscape that is still full of texture and character.

Low-growing shrubs, including junipers and cotoneasters, flank the front steps of a Long Island house (opposite). Cedar shingles stained red, then softened with gray, cast a faint mauve glow in the twilight. A garage and pergola enclose a neat backyard (above), helping to create a sense of privacy and order. The carefully cultivated lawn is an inviting expanse of open space beyond the tall, carefree shore grasses.

Young trees, including white birch, black pine, and purple-leaf plum, introduce contrasting colors and seasonal interest to the front yard (right). All are well suited to the damp seaside climate. A newly planted wildflower meadow fronts the property. After years of tilling and farming, the well-composted soil required no additives; the seeds, broadcasted and kept well watered, took two seasons before producing flowering plants.

Columns add a classical touch to a wraparound porch (left) without detracting from the low-key, country character of the house. The planted border features Montauk daisies about to burst into bloom. Regional favorites, these perennials are low-maintenance fall bloomers that grow particularly well near the seashore.

A graceful backyard pergola (right) echoes the classical theme of the house. The ready-made hardwood columns are identical to those on the front porch and link the two structures visually. The purple wisteria took three years to flower. Seven to fifteen years often pass before the woody vines begin blooming, but sandy soil seems to encourage an earlier bloom.

GRASS ROOTS

For many gardeners, no yard is complete without a lush expanse of green grass. Beautiful lawns, however, don't just happen. The work begins before the first seed is sown, when it is necessary to assess the property's moisture level and take note of how much sun or shade it receives.

Then the grass must be selected accordingly. Two basic types are used for lawns: cool-season and warm-season. Cool-season grasses, good for Northern climates, stay green in the winter but may turn brown in very hot, dry weather. These are generally planted in mixtures, and include Kentucky bluegrass, fine fescues, perennial rye grass, and bent grass. They can be put in either as seed or as sod, and are best mowed high.

Warm-season varieties, including Bermuda grass, St. Augustine grass, zoysia grass, and carpet grass, stay green in hot weather but go dormant in winter. As a result, they are good for Southern climates, but not recommended for the North. Warm-season grasses are generally used individually and started as plugs or sod; they are best mowed close.

While they produce fine-textured lawns, many specialized grasses require up to three times the amount of rain expected to fall in a given region. Lower-thirst hybrids, however, are constantly being improved. In the cool-season group, consider the water-saving turf-type tall fescues; warm-season options that need less watering include shade-tolerant Bahia grass, sun-loving buffalo grass, and blue grama grass.

Whatever the type, healthy grass needs proper care and feeding. A high-nitrogen fertilizer should be applied twice a year, in spring and fall. If a weed-killer is necessary, opt for a low-toxic type such as glyphosate, which has a short-term residual impact. Another rule of thumb: Never mow a wet lawn. It is not only difficult, as the grass will lie flat, but also produces a ragged cut.

Country in the City

For urban gardeners, the question is nearly universal: How can a featureless yard be given the appeal of a country bower? A Denver, Colorado, family succeeded in this long, narrow garden, which was transformed by a burst of annuals and perennials and an imaginatively painted shed that lends a personal sense of whimsy.

Making the most of the space, which is seventy feet long, the owners restricted flowers to a single border running along a brick side wall, leaving room for their young daughters' baseball and soccer games in an open lawn beside it. A full eight feet wide, the dramatic flower border was planted in the style of an English cottage garden, with perennials, annuals, herbs, and roses mixed together for a wonderfully romantic, untamed look. Favorite blues dominated the painterly palette, enriched by accents of silver, yellow, and salmon pink. Special attention was also paid to fragrance and interacting shapes; for added interest, the plants were staggered in height throughout the bed, and set off by a row of green junipers.

As in many good gardens, the design has evolved in stages. One year after planting, for example, the border was full, but still required more autumn planting to extend the blooming season into August and September. Thus, to the existing delphiniums, lady's mantle, Russian sage, chamomile, and painted daisies, the owners added lilies, including Aurelian Trumpet and Oriental hybrids, as well as perennial asters, boltonias, and heleniums.

Once a successful planting scheme was established, the familiar problem of limited storage space still remained. As for most gardens, a vast collection of pots, tools, and other paraphernalia needed a home. The answer, quite logically, was a toolshed, but for these owners, no ordinary building would do.

A Colorado garden (above) offers fantasy and tranquillity in an urban setting. The long herbaceous border features blue- and silver-colored plants, including irises, blue flax, campanulas, delphiniums, Corsican violets, lavender, and lamb's ears. Peonies, poppies, roses, and lilies provide accents of white, yellow, and salmon pink. Clever trompe l'oeil painting turned an ordinary plywood toolshed (opposite) into a special garden feature.

FISHER & CHAPPELL
SEED CO.
75¢
FISHER &

Opting for a simple, inexpensive design, they built a plain plywood structure measuring nine feet square, with a cedar-shingle roof and poured concrete floor. Then came the fun: Collaboration with two local artists yielded a witty trompe l'oeil, or "fool-the-eye," painted design for the exterior. The challenge was to create the illusion of an ivy-covered garden shed that would look as if it had been in place for years, but that also had a sense of humor.

To relate it to the main house, a formal 1920s brick Georgian Revival, the small shed gained some distinguishing architectural details with the flash of a paintbrush, including the "stone" lintel over the window and projecting quoins at its corners. Ensuring a natural look in both winter and summer, evergreen ivy and a small, red-berried shrub, rather than flowers, were chosen for the painted foundation "planting." But the clever design didn't stop there: Lighthearted touches include a straw hat hanging from a shutter, a jacket slung casually on a peg rack, and a composite portrait of the owners' two daughters. The designs look so deceptively real that only a second glance reveals them to be brushwork.

The care given to the creation of this imaginative shed is indicative of the owners' close involvement with the entire project. "We've taken great pleasure in designing and working in our little yard," they say. "Our garden reflects ourselves: It may be urban in reality, but it's country at heart."

Fool-the-eye seed packets stay forever safely tucked into an equally realistic French-style shutter (opposite top left). Whimsical painted creatures include a Rocky Mountain woodpecker (opposite top right), perched on clinging vines of ivy, which are real – or are they? Other flights of painterly fancy include a portrait of one owner's garden boots (opposite). From the nearby watering can, a frog prince surveys the scene. Below him, painted foliage merges with genuine violas, further obscuring the line between fantasy and reality.

FOOLING THE EYE

Decorative painting known as *trompe l'oeil*, in which a flat rendering creates the illusion of three dimensions, has its roots in ancient Egyptian, Greek, and Roman murals. The technique was first used to solve an architectural problem or to create a sense of architecture where none existed, but has since been expanded to encompass an almost limitless range of whimsical elements.

Popular trompe l'oeil techniques today include sponging or ragging on color to create the textured look of stone or stucco, as well as detailed pictorial handwork. For gardens, finishes that simulate copper verdigris or bronze work well on plaques, statues, fountains, lanterns, and weathervanes.

When working outdoors, it is important to choose weather-resistant, colorfast primers, paints, and stains. The artists who painted the potting shed on these pages worked with latex exterior house paint, sponging five layers of color onto the primed plywood to simulate old stucco plaster. The basic shapes of vines, bricks, and shrubs were carefully stenciled on, then filled in freehand with more details and shadows.

Old birdhouses and a picnic basket top a primitive cupboard in the shed (opposite). The shed is used to ready plants for the outdoors, but it has proved an inviting retreat at all times – especially in the rain. The owners' children love it too, and consider the cozy space a playhouse of sorts, devoted to the art of growing things. A scrub-top table (above) holds a still life of scented geraniums, miniature roses, alpine strawberries, rosemary, a potted melon vine, and, for tying herbs, a length of gardening twine. A basket of petunias and lobelias sits in a vintage French wicker chair (right).

A Garden Railway

Some gardeners go beyond the mere cultivation of plants to express a particular hobby or interest. In Colorado, the owners of this remarkable theme garden, known as a garden railway, have produced a very personal landscape that combines their individual pursuits. His interest in trains and railroad travel and hers in plants and miniatures merge splendidly in the 36-by-50-foot yard of their 1924 stucco-covered bungalow.

The couple became intrigued with garden railways on numerous visits to England. It was there that these small-scale worlds originated, evolving from a popular interest in model trains that paralleled the development of the railroad industry from the mid-nineteenth century onward. Model trains were often exact replicas of their full-size counterparts, and it wasn't long before both children and adults – captivated by this new advancement in transportation – began collecting diminutive engines and all their accoutrements.

Few families, however, had the space inside their homes for extensive train layouts, so they moved the engines and tracks outdoors. While some railway gardens were quite modest, the vogue reached its height on Britain's large estates, where detailed complexes complete with bridges, station houses, passengers, and yards and yards of track wound their way through intricate miniature landscapes.

By the middle of this century, enthusiasm for garden railways had waned, but in 1969, a German company introduced plastic model railroad sets designed specifically for outdoor use. It is to these all-weather trains that railway gardening owes its current revival. Today's engines may be electric, battery powered, or driven by steam, and can run through rain and snow. The surrounding terrain, scaled to suit the trains, is likely

A garden railway (opposite) was inspired by similar theme gardens popular in England. Among the plants are many alpine varieties, which do well in an arid climate; their small scale also suits the trains. Santolina displays its yellow flowers behind a child's watering can, while purple lavender thrives to the right of the station house. The locomotive (above left) is of British make, while the railbus is a one-of-a-kind model designed by its owner. A full-size switch stand (above right) is an unusual but especially appropriate garden ornament.

A miniature live-steam locomotive pulls handmade wooden freightcars through the garden (right). Plants to the right of the sidewalk are 'Munstead' lavender, tall pink asters behind, and blooming oregano that trails onto the path. A low hedge of pine-leaf penstemon borders the track. Trees to the left of the sidewalk include dwarf golden arborvitae, dwarf Norway spruce, and a large white lilac. The purple blooms behind the train are Nierembergia 'Purple Robe'. Dwarf zinnias and sweet alyssum are scattered throughout.

to feature herbs, miniature Dutch bulbs, and dwarf conifers, as well as alpine plants.

In creating this garden, the owners first collected their trains, which represent a variety of makes but which all run on dual-gauge track (nos. 1 and 0). After establishing the plan on paper, they constructed the track by hand, using redwood ties and brass rails that retain a natural appearance even after years of weathering. Once the garden site was leveled – a task essential to a smooth-running train – the 104-foot track loop went down piece by piece on a bed of crushed granite.

The plantings were designed equally carefully. The smallest perennials found their place closest to tracks, bridges, and buildings – scaled one half inch to one foot – while larger species were set back to form a backdrop. "Some plants were used as single specimens, some were grouped in natural-looking drifts, and still others were lined up as miniature hedges for bits of formality or border definition here and there," one owner explains. Pine-leaf penstemon, for example, found a natural home next to the main line, forming a small-scale hedge that provides year-round texture and color. A thick planting of 'Munstead' dwarf lavender serves a similar function along a brick path.

The completion of this unusual miniature world was appropriately celebrated with a ribbon-cutting ceremony and the driving of a golden spike made by a friend who is a jeweler. Say the owners, "We now know how the builders of the Transcontinental Railroad must have felt!"

"Sammy," an English live-steam locomotive by Archangel, pulls passenger coaches over a trestle bridge (top left). Spring flowers include grape hyacinths and budding Oriental poppies. Locomotives from Japan, America, and Germany let off some steam (center left) amid tufts of blue fescue grass and portulaca. Down by the tracks (bottom left), passengers both young and old gossip and wait for the next train. The engine, screened by a lush border of Kamchatka sedum, is an American Shay.

Shelley, the family's box turtle, makes her way down the tracks (right). A combination of woolly thyme and silver variegated thyme forms a thick ground cover, while germander, English lavender, and bright-yellow yarrow bloom in the background. The windmill, measuring just over a foot high, was made from a kit.

Working for Pleasure

In Northern California's Sonoma County, one enterprising couple has found a way to turn their love of plants into a way of life. Their wholesale nursery and cut-flower farm in the heart of fertile vineyard country keeps them involved with gardening on a year-round, full-time basis.

Awake at five o'clock and in the fields by six, the two follow a demanding schedule. But their days are satisfying, and they are fortunate to be able to draw on their individual strengths and interests for their work: He's an economist and horticulturist, she's an accomplished floral designer. With fields and greenhouses in which to roam, the couple's four children benefit from the family enterprise as well.

Although about 90 employees help maintain the 114-acre farm, decisions regarding production, marketing strategy, and the introduction of new varieties fall to the couple. Since the commute from the family's 100-year-old farmhouse to the nursery takes less than

Ready for arrangements, cut roses (above) include the all-yellow grandiflora 'Gold Medal,' the soft-pink floribunda 'Pleasure,' and the coral-hued hybrid tea 'Voodoo.' The stems of gaura, an easy-to-grow perennial, are ideal filler for bouquets.

Roses are parked temporarily in the kitchen (opposite), on their way to the local flower market. A broad veranda on the family's farmhouse offers an enticing view of field after field of roses (overleaf).

five minutes, they are able to stay near their children but can be on hand quickly when problems arise.

Care of the gardens is a main priority. The hundreds of container-grown perennials, ornamental trees, and shrubs take up 50 acres alone, and would cause almost anyone to pause for a second glance. But the roses ~ field upon field of them ~ are perhaps the most striking sight. More than 60 varieties of hybrid teas, floribundas, miniatures, and old-fashioned favorites are raised on the farm. Those that aren't sold to San Francisco merchants are cut and carted off to two 9,000-square-foot flower barns on the premises. There, a range of blossoms, along with a variety of fragrant herbs, are dried and find a second life in natural-looking arrangements and wreaths.

Indeed, roses are the family's specialty, and years of trial and error have convinced these seasoned gardeners to question what they read in catalogues. "The ratings provided for roses do not always reflect how individual varieties will grow in specific regions of the country," they caution. "To know their suitability to your own garden, you really need to try them yourself."

The couple encourage inexperienced rose growers to look carefully at established gardens in their own areas to see which plants do well, and perhaps to experiment with a few proven winners. 'Iceberg,' a white floribunda, 'Tournament of Roses,' a warm-pink hybrid tea rose, and the grandiflora 'Gold Medal' are good choices for most parts of the country, and all are disease resistant.

Dried arrangements (opposite) include a bouquet of santolina, tied with French ribbon (top left); a heart-shaped wreath of garden roses and daffodils on a Spanish moss base (center left); and sheaves of wheat secured with raffia (bottom left). Fragrance logs (far right), made of lavender, dill, sage, and scented geraniums, are ready to toss into the fireplace.

EVERLASTINGS

Drying flowers for wreaths and other arrangements is a wonderful way to preserve the essence of a garden through all the seasons. Below are some suggested drying methods; different flowers and colors produce different results, so it is a good idea to test each approach.

Air drying: Secure bunched stems with twine or rubber bands and suspend head down from a clothesline or drying rack in a well-ventilated room, out of direct sunlight.

Microwave: Spread cuttings on a paper towel and heat at a low setting for one to three minutes, depending on the fleshiness of the plants.

Dessicant: Immerse cuttings in silica-gel crystals for one to three days, or in fine builder's sand for one to three weeks, depending on the humidity of the room and the fleshiness of the plants.

For a list of flowers suggested for drying, see the Plant Lists at the back of the book.

AGERATUM
PHLOX
TALL

chapter three

FLOWERS, TREES & SHRUBS

The key to the success of any country garden lies in the judicious choice of plants, which will set the mood you want and help your gardening dreams bloom into reality. The selection of varieties that will suit a country setting is almost limitless, however, and choosing well means understanding the plants' individual needs. Some, for example, have a strong preference for acid rather than alkaline soil, or do best grown under moist, rather than dry, conditions. Some, too, will withstand city air better than others, or thrive in shade as opposed to sun.

This chapter offers an overview of garden plants, including the trees and shrubs that shape the framework of a landscape, along with annuals and perennials, vegetables and herbs, bulbs, ground covers, vines, ornamental grasses, and water plants. Becoming familiar with their various characteristics will help you lay the groundwork for a flourishing country garden of your own, and learning how they can mix and work together will ensure pleasure throughout all the seasons.

The Cornerstones ~ Trees & Shrubs

Trees and shrubs set the stage for a garden. As the most permanent living elements in a landscape, they can establish the good "bones" of a design, and their placement has a strong influence on other growth. These living garden fixtures are also important for providing mass, texture, and shade, and for functioning as sound barriers, windbreaks, and natural privacy screens. Moreover, many species offer food and shelter to birds and insects that are valuable for pollinating plants.

Flowering in the early spring, the Bradford pear (opposite) is a deciduous tree favored for its pleasing pyramidal shape, white blooms, and glossy green leaves. It grows 30 to 50 feet tall, bears tiny ornamental fruits, and is more resistant than other varieties to fire blight, a bacterial disease particularly destructive to pear trees. Come fall, the foliage turns shades of red ranging from bright crimson to deep burgundy. When used well, trees and shrubs can work hard to help shape a landscape (above), defining and enclosing a yard, while providing dimension to background views.

By definition, a tree is a woody perennial that stands on its own, has a single trunk, and grows to a height of at least 12 to 15 feet at maturity. In contrast to soft-stemmed herbaceous perennials, which die back to ground level each winter, trees remain intact through the cold months, albeit in a dormant state. This dormancy is apparent when deciduous trees lose their leaves in autumn.

Evergreen trees, on the other hand, retain their leaves for at least one full-year cycle, even during dormancy. The term "evergreen" is somewhat of a misnomer, as many varieties yield foliage in colors other than green. Broadleaf evergreens ~ magnolias, live oaks, eucalyptus, olives, and hollies ~ have flat leaves similar to those of deciduous trees. Yet, because they

hold their foliage for a year and produce new growth as necessary, they never appear to lose their leaves. Narrow-leaf evergreens ~ including spruces, pines, cedars, arborvitaes, hemlocks, and firs ~ also retain their needle-like or scaly leaves for a year or more. These trees are called conifers because they bear woody or berry-like cones filled with seeds. Larch (or tamarack) trees, bald cypresses, and dawn redwoods are exceptions to these categories, as they are deciduous cone-bearing, narrow-leaf evergreens.

Shrubs are also woody perennials, generally smaller than trees, with several trunks or stems; many can be trained to grow as single-trunk plants so that they look

A quartet of crabapple trees laden with deep pink blossoms arch over billowing hedges of boxwood (above). Crabapple trees bear diminutive fruits too tart to eat raw but ideal for canning and for making applesauce, jelly, cider, and juice. The deciduous star magnolia (opposite top) grows about 15 feet high and bears a profusion of fragrant white double blooms in spring. Although this is one of the hardiest magnolias, the blooms may be nipped by frost if the plant is not placed in a protected area. The Yulan magnolia (opposite bottom left) bears large, scented white flowers. In contrast, evergreen magnolias bear flowers along with their leaves; the 'Bechtel' crabapple (opposite bottom right) emits a delightful fragrance.

like trees. Some shrubs, slightly tender for their climate, will die back to the ground in winter, to emerge the following spring. Shrubs, like trees, are categorized as deciduous (weigelas, dogwoods, spireas) or broadleaf evergreens (firethorns, andromedas, camellias, some rhododendrons, azaleas, and laurels). Others are coniferous evergreens such as yews and junipers. Within each group there are diverse levels of hardiness and regional preferences. Junipers tend to be hardy all over the United States, for example, while rhododendrons thrive in the Northeast and Northwest; azaleas grow best in the South.

To choose shrubs and trees successfully means considering their various qualities. Ornamental varieties, for example, might be favored for their fruits, colorful fall foliage, or unusual bark. Flowers, of course, are another attribute: Nothing could be more satisfying, for example, than the abundance of huge, showy blossoms that hydrangeas will yield with a minimum of effort. Numerous trees and shrubs are also endowed with delightful fragrances.

Form is another important characteristic. Certain trees and shrubs are especially suitable for hedging. In addition to neatly trimmed boxwoods and privets, there are many informal-looking varieties, including shrub roses, heaths, and deutzias. Shaping espaliers is also a way to create a striking screen or hedge; particularly elegant effects can be created with firethorns, pears, apples, and other fruit trees trained on a frame or wall. Topiary, the art of sculpting shrubs and trees into fanciful shapes, is a very effective use of such plants as yew, hemlock, and rosemary.

A sinuous border of snow azaleas (opposite) helps create a bold composition in a wooded garden. This fragrant evergreen azalea from Japan is exceptionally hardy, growing well from Long Island southward. Because it is so dense, it lends itself well to hedging.

PLANTING SHRUBS FOR COLOR

While shrubs are often relegated to practical duty as "foundation" plants, they can actually contribute as much as flowers to the decorative impact of a landscape. Whether chosen for their showy blooms or fruit, distinctive seasonal foliage, or unusual branch formations, these versatile plants will provide interest and color to a garden throughout the year.

Many shrubs, such as the springtime favorite forsythia, stand out with a relatively brief but brilliant burst of bloom, then blend into the background when their blossoms fade. Other spring-blooming shrubs, however, continue to show off, following their flowers with handsome summer foliage, then fruit, and perhaps a brilliant turn of fall color; this is particularly true of quinces and many viburnums.

But the drama doesn't have to stop with autumn. Evergreen shrubs, like hollies, for example, provide distinctive color and texture throughout the coldest months, as do winter-blooming species such as goat willows and witch hazels. Those with unique branch formations, like curly hazelnut, and shrubs with ornamental berries, such as the red-fruited chokeberry, are also welcome showpieces against a gray winter background.

For a list of shrubs that provide seasonal color, see the Plant Lists at the back of the book.

PLANTING TREES AND SHRUBS

When purchased from a nursery, shrubs and trees generally come in one of three basic forms: bare-root, container-grown, or with soil-bound roots tightly wrapped in burlap (B & B, or balled and burlapped). Each type has individual planting requirements, but as a rule of thumb, all need a generous hole at least three times wider than the root spread and one-and-a-half times as deep as the container or root ball. The soil from the hole should be amended with one part peat moss to two parts loam; this will help aerate it and retain moisture.

To plant, shovel the amended soil back into the hole until it is one-third full and tamp the dirt down firmly to prevent the tree or shrub from settling too low, which can kill it. Then place the plant in the hole. Adjust the bottom soil layer until the original soil mark on the trunk aligns with the ground. Heavy clay or silt soils may "give" more than sandy soils, so plant slightly high with these types.

When the level is set, gently spread the roots inside the hole, and cut away any broken bits or roots near the base of the trunk that might strangle the plant. It is also important to remove all container material, including the pressed-fiber pots meant to rot away in the soil after planting. These can suffocate the roots before the container has time to decay. On B & B plants, the twine should be cut and the burlap peeled about one-third back around the plant. (If wire or synthetic material is used, cut away as much as possible.) You can guard against planting B & Bs too deeply by establishing the true juncture of the trunk and roots beneath the burlap and situating plants accordingly. When the plant is positioned, fill the hole with the remaining soil, tamping it to the root-trunk juncture at ground level. (Keep the juncture slightly higher in clay-based soils.) Water immediately and thoroughly, and add mulch.

The spring-blooming common lilac (opposite) yields exceptionally fragrant flower clusters in tandem with its heart-shaped leaves. Related to both the olive and the privet, this shrub was introduced to Europe in the sixteenth century from Turkey. It was a favorite with American Colonists, and was planted widely throughout New England. The late-spring blossoms of the wayfaring tree (above left) gleam against its deep-green, textured leaves. Native to Great Britain, the wayfaring tree is said to have been planted alongside cow sheds to protect against witchcraft. This tree-like shrub belongs to the viburnum family, a group of plants well suited for massing in a shrub border. In fall, it bears yellow and red berries that gradually turn black (opposite above right).

Whatever their type, trees and shrubs require careful siting. Shrubs grow more rapidly than trees do, and, if planted too closely together, may require pruning, which will interfere with their natural shape and beauty. Shrubs and trees should be placed away from utility and irrigation lines, and those types that drop fruit or drip sap are best situated far from a seating area such as a terrace.

It is also important to allow plenty of room for mature height and breadth. Roots, which may spread beyond three times the distance of the drip line of the outermost branches, tend to form most densely in the top two feet of garden soil. Thus, any adjacent plants will have to

The big-leaf hydrangea (above and left) is well loved for its large clusters of sterile blooms, which are borne in summer. Variations in color make it a popular flower for cutting and an excellent candidate for dried arrangements. (Acidic soil produces blue flowers while neutral or alkaline conditions yield pink and red.) The plants should be pruned immediately after flowering, as they bear flowers on the previous year's growth. The corymbs of a Lacecap hydrangea (opposite) combine the large sterile flowers with smaller, fertile ones. There are many other varieties and cultivars available, including oak-leaf and climbing hydrangeas. Most prefer rich, moist soil and partial or full sun.

compete for water and sunlight. Eventually, the roots will extend beyond an area that is practical to maintain, so the plants should already be naturally suited to the soil's acid level, density, and drainage capacity.

Novice gardeners may be nervous about planting trees and shrubs, but the task is actually relatively simple as long as there are enough people on hand to help lift and place the heavy root balls. (Plants should be lifted only by the pots or root balls, and never held by the branches or trunks.)

Once the shrub or tree is settled in the ground, it is best not to prune the top third of the plant as is commonly suggested, although any broken limbs, dual leaders, and ingrowing branches that interfere with the basic shape should be trimmed. Subsequent pruning will vary with different kinds of trees, shrubs, and hedges, as will fertilizing. Most evergreens, for example, recover better from transplanting if they are not fertilized immediately.

The Passion for Roses

No other flower challenges the beauty and fragrance of the rose. Known to exist for millions of years, this versatile family of shrubby plants contains members probably more widely raised than any other garden flower. This is largely the result of a complex process of hybridization over the past century or so that has produced countless named varieties, many of which have been developed for extra hardiness and an extended blooming season.

The estimated 20,000 rose cultivars currently named have been crossbred from eight Asiatic species roses, which are the original varieties found in the wild. Most hybrids including miniatures and climbers developed from the mid-nineteenth century onward are known as modern roses, and include the familiar Hybrid Teas, formally introduced with 'La France' in 1867. Characterized by good repeat flowering and brilliant colors, these, in turn, were crossed in the early 1900s with Polyantha roses to create the heavily blooming Floribunda varieties. Hybrid Teas were also subsequently crossed with Floribundas to produce tall, vigorous Grandifloras.

Roses developed before the mid-1800s are generally known as old-fashioned roses and include species roses and older hybrids and variations. Among them are Polyanthas, Chinas, Gallicas, Damasks, Bourbons, and Centifolias, or Cabbage Roses. Prized for their wonderful fragrance, vigor, and splendid blossoms, old garden and species roses are currently undergoing a revival.

An extravagant cluster of warm-hued modern roses (opposite) includes the yellow Grandiflora 'Gold Medal,' the orange Hybrid Tea 'Voodoo,' the pink Hybrid Tea 'Bewitched,' and the ivory Floribunda 'French Lace.' A still life of old-fashioned roses (above) shows off the full, double-petaled forms that distinguish them from many of their modern counterparts.

The pink-edged petals of the popular climbing Hybrid Tea 'Peace' stand out in stark relief against a background of marigolds (opposite top left). The divided petals of 'Souvenir de la Malmaison' (opposite top right), a sumptuous Bourbon rose dating from 1843, exhibit the quartered appearance that characterizes some of the old garden types. The fragrant Hybrid Tea 'Princesse de Monaco' (opposite bottom left) is a vigorous bush rose. 'Americana' (opposite bottom right) is another richly colored variety of Hybrid Tea. 'Fortune's Double Yellow' (right), a once-blooming climbing rose, was discovered in China in 1845 by the Scottish botanist Robert Fortune. A tender rose, it has distinctive apple-green foliage that makes the plant handsome even when not in bloom. Shown climbing, this apricot-hued rose can also be grown freestanding.

Foxglove

Exuberant Perennials

Few denizens of the garden offer the exuberance of perennials. Returning year after year, perennials are noted for their vast array of highly decorative flowers and distinct blooming periods. Many are also shade tolerant, an attribute that increases the already astonishing versatility of a plant group that may be used in beds or as spreading ground covers, or naturalized in woodland, prairie, wetland, desert, and alpine areas.

Many perennials grow well in pots; a peach-leaved bellflower, a type of campanula, shares quarters with tall pink foxglove (opposite). Perennials can be planted to bloom simultaneously in vivid color combinations. The purple-blue blossoms of the ornamental perennial flax contrast with the lustrous red of Icelandic poppies (above left). Veronicas, (above right) are also known as speedwells. They are relatives of the snapdragon, and are valued for their long blooming period. Cultivars of veronica flower in blue, pink, violet, and white.

Most garden perennials are "herbaceous," which means their stems are soft, rather than woody like a shrub's. Herbaceous perennials bloom for more than one season, differing from annuals, which live and die within one growing season, and from biennials, which grow foliage their first season, then bloom and die the following year. Some perennials tend to be relatively short-lived, like violas, which can die after just a year or two. But others - peonies, for instance - have been known to flourish for generations.

In winter, herbaceous perennials die back to the ground, but their tough, often spreading roots live through the season to send forth new shoots in the spring. It is this method of regeneration that distinguishes perennials from annuals and biennials.

Although a number of perennials will set seed dependably, others do so only infrequently; it is more

effective to multiply by means of their root systems. The major advantage of these root propagators is that they can reproduce vegetatively, rather than by seed only. This means that their rootstocks or stems may be divided or cut to produce plants identical to the parent. Ideal seasons for dividing perennials are dictated by species and hardiness zone, but dividing every third year is a good rule of thumb.

To create a garden with lasting color, it is a good idea to plan perennial beds carefully. An easy way to design a succession of blooms is to diagram the different plants on separate sheets of tracing paper according to when they flower. Four overlays can be placed over the garden-bed plan to denote spring, summer, fall, and winter. In this manner, it is possible to establish the duration of bloom in each section. Planting in large drifts of one species is more effective than dotting single specimens helter-skelter. A simple plan with prolonged, harmonious blooming periods is always better than a complex mix that produces scattered, brief bursts of color.

A pair of Scotties frolic in a patch of snow-in-summer (above left). This ground-covering perennial grows into woolly mats of grayish-green foliage covered with small white flowers in early summer. Multiplying rapidly, snow-in-summer can be invasive, but it is ideal for rock gardens and will even grow in sand. Black-eyed Susans (above), late-summer bloomers also called rudbeckias, show off in front of a growth of cleomes, which are annuals. In a carefree perennial garden (opposite), ornamental grasses blend with bluish-green artemisia, tender verbenas, and yellow-blooming rabbitbrush. Such grasses provide decorative interest throughout the year.

When a perennial border is sited against a wall or shrubbery, an aisle at least three feet wide should be left between the plants and the background to allow for weeding and air circulation. An edging between bed and lawn will permit plants to overflow a bit without being damaged by a mower.

Most perennials grow well in rich, loamy soil with good drainage and benefit from periodic amendment with organic matter. Usually, they favor slightly acidic to neutral soil. Both clay-based and sandy soils should be improved with the addition of a two- to four-inch layer of peat moss, leaf mold, compost, or well-rotted manure. The best fertilizers for perennial planting are those low in nitrogen but high in phosphorous and potassium, to help establish roots.

Perennials are sold as container or bare-root plants. Container perennials need generous holes and are best planted to the same depth as they are in their pots. Bare-root plants should be planted to the soil marks on the stems, with the roots spread over a mound of soil in the base of the hole to prevent air pockets. A reputable nursery can provide specific information on fertilizing and planting times.

Most perennials, of course, also can be cultivated from seed, and catalogs offer a generous assortment to choose from. A two- to three-year wait is necessary before the first blooms appear.

Distinguished by fern-like foliage, painted daisies complement the delicate blooms of coral bells (opposite left). Members of the chrysanthemum family, these summer-blooming daisies come in pink, white, red, or lilac, and are excellent for cutting. False dragonheads, or obedient plants (opposite right), burst forth in late summer or fall. Highly versatile perennials, they range from two to four feet tall, and thrive in sun or shade and in any type of soil. Painted daisies (top left) show off their rose-pink petals and yellow button centers. A lucky ladybug investigates a snow-in-summer blossom (above right). This welcome garden visitor devours aphids and other pests. Commonly known as pincushion flowers, sun-loving scabiosas (bottom left) bear blue, lavender, mauve, or white blossoms on two-foot-tall stems. This perennial will bloom from summer through fall if the faded flowers are snipped off. Columbine (bottom right) produces exquisite blooms, often with long, showy spurs. It is well suited to partially shaded rock gardens and perennial borders.

THE GREAT COVER-UP

Spreading horizontally in quick-growing masses, perennial ground covers are great boons where grass is difficult to grow, and are excellent for low-maintenance areas where mowing is impractical.

Ground covers embrace many types of plants, including those that are shade-tolerant, hardy, and evergreen. While they are all spreaders, these useful plants grow in a variety of ways. Some, like junipers, yews, roses, and cotoneasters, are essentially low shrubs. Others, including hostas and daylilies, are clump-forming, and expand from a main rootstock. Still others, among them periwinkles and thyme, send out long runners or prostrate stems to create a carpet-like covering. Vines, on the other hand, generally cling with tendrils or rootlets. Many vines start as ground covers but climb once they find vertical support; this is true of English Ivy, five-leaf akebia, euonymus, and honeysuckle.

For a list of ground covers, see the Plant Lists at the back of the book.

The Charm of Flowering Bulbs

Best known as the cheery harbingers of spring, flowering bulbs are actually available for every season and climate. The "bulb" itself is a modified food storage system and takes a variety of forms: true bulbs (narcissi, lilies, and tulips) and corms (crocuses and gladioli), which are both essentially swollen underground stems; tuberous roots (dahlias); rhizomes (cannas and irises); and tuber-corms (tuberous begonias, anemones, and ranunculuses).

Many bulbs require cold conditions during their dormant period in order to bloom properly, and all need to continue growing after flowering until their leaves turn yellow and die back. This allows the bulb to store food so it can nurture the following year's growth.

Most bulb plants do best in sunny locations and should be planted at a depth approximately two-and-a-half times their diameter in rich, sandy loam; good drainage is essential to prevent rotting and disease. Some bulb plants, including daffodils, grape hyacinths, and squills, are especially suitable for naturalizing in lawns and meadows or on the edges of wooded areas. Others, like tulips and lilies, are better adapted for planting in beds.

True bulbs such as narcissus are left in the ground throughout the year, while tender corms like gladiolus are dug up and stored for the winter. Given the proper conditions, all bulbs will bloom throughout the year, from the earliest spring snowdrops and cyclamens to summer-blooming lilies and autumn montbretias; bulb flowers like amaryllis and paperwhites can also be "forced" to bloom indoors during winter months.

Named after the Greek goddess of the rainbow, the iris is one of the most popular of all bulb plants. The tall purple variety (opposite) is of the bearded rhizomatous type, characterized by fuzzy falls, or hanging petals. It is available in countless cultivars, sizes, and colors. These dramatic flowers look beautiful on their own, but blend equally well into perennial borders. Double narcissus (above) are extremely fragrant and excellent multipliers.

The pristine white cactus dahlia (opposite top left) is from a family of tuberous-rooted herbs native to Mexico. In all but the most temperate climates, the tuberous roots of summer- and fall-blooming dahlias must be dug up and stored in a cool dry place before the danger of frost. They can be replanted the following spring. Mauve colchicums (opposite top right), or fall-blooming crocus, grow from corms planted in the summer. The blushing trumpets of the Regal lily (opposite bottom left) exhale a rich perfume; can reach six feet in height. The scented white umbels of garlic chives (opposite bottom right) are grown from bulbs belonging to the allium family. The huge, globe-shaped flower heads of giant purple alliums (right) are among the most decorative of the late spring-flowering bulbs.

Soothing Water Gardens

Whether it is trickling from a fountain, tumbling through a stream bed, or gleaming serenely in a pool, water adds a different dimension of pleasure to the garden. When it is moving, it provides soothing sounds and sensations, and when it is still, its surface acts like a mirror to extend views and record a changing picture of the seasons as they come and go.

Ponds and water gardens also provide for a large family of plants. There are numerous types of aquatic plants in addition to the familiar water lilies and lotuses. These include bog, or marginal, plants such as water irises, bulrushes, and cattails, which congregate on or along the water's edge. Bog plants root in soil under shallow water but can extend their foliage above the surface. Other water plants are floaters, while still others, like elodea, live submerged and help oxygenate the water around them.

It is possible to create an environment for water-loving plants in almost any setting, even if there are no existing natural bodies of water. Many types and shapes of containers will accommodate small, portable aquatic gardens in diverse climates. Flexible vinyl or polyethylene pool liners are ideal for creating pool shapes to fit the contours of a particular site.

Whatever the shape or size, the depth of a water garden should meet the needs of the resident plants and animals, providing space below the frost line for any that are wintering over. Most aquatic plants prefer a sunny exposure, and clean water free of leaves.

While the flowers and foliage of the fragrant Sacred lotus (above left) float on the water, the plant actually roots in bottom soil. Lotuses are hardy, easy-to-grow plants, prized for their mid-summer blooms and their decorative seed pods. A relative of the lotus, the Royal Purple water lily (above right) displays a vivid hue characteristic of tropical types. Including day and night bloomers, tropical water lilies flower from mid-summer to frost. Japanese irises (opposite) grow splendidly on the banks of a small stream. This type of rhizomatous, beardless iris flowers in a wide range of colors.

Hard-Working Annuals

Annuals are plants that reproduce primarily from seed and fulfill their life span within a single year's growing season. Rapid and prolific bloomers, they can provide masses of instant color to any landscape. Seasoned gardeners know that the more these satisfying plants are cut, the more they will blossom in their attempt to set seed. Indeed, sown from just a few packets of seeds, annuals produce impressive results, whether they are strategically placed to fill in between perennials, scattered in a cutting garden of their own, or grown in containers.

Although annuals do not return from rootstock year after year as perennials do, growing plants from seed is economical and gives gardeners plenty of opportunity to experiment from season to season with different varieties of flowers. Most annuals perform best in full sun, and most favor neutral soil enriched with organic matter.

Depending on their germination habits and on how tolerant the plants are to cold and heat, annuals are categorized in hardy, half-hardy, tender, and heat-resistant subclasses. The particular subclass, in turn, dictates whether an annual should be grown from seed or introduced to a garden as a seedling or more established plant. It is a good idea to read the packets carefully to determine if seeds should be sown early in pots indoors or if they may be planted directly in the ground. When seeding or transplanting annuals outdoors, it is also important to wait until the last hard spring frost has passed.

Bedding pansies (opposite) find a happy home in a wooden tub. A type of viola, pansies are actually perennials but are treated as hardy annuals. They flourish in cool weather, and some varieties may be sown or bedded as very young plants in the fall; protected with mulch, they will emerge the following spring. In extremely cold areas, though, they fare better with early spring planting. Ribbons of golden coleus, gray-green dusty miller, and purple ageratum, all grown as annuals, create a dramatic grouping (above left). Cosmos (above right), an annual member of the daisy family, blooms in a range of hues, including white, yellow, orange, and crimson. This cheerful flower does well in hot climates.

LOW-MAINTENANCE ANNUALS

By choosing annuals that germinate quickly from seed, have prolonged periods of bloom, and are well suited to the local climate, any gardener can produce a season's worth of blooms with little trouble.

An easy annual garden is best cultivated with plants that require minimum watering, are pest-resistant, and grow thickly enough to suppress weeds and create masses of color. Whether they are used alone or as companions to perennials, many annuals will perform well until the first hard frost. A natural organic fertilizer such as fish emulsion will help new transplants adapt and provide a boost for annuals planted in containers; a light mulch will keep weeds at bay from seedlings. Young plants benefit from thinning, which prevents overcrowding and reduces competition for light, water, and air. Deep watering is usually more effective and time-efficient than superficial, frequent sprinklings.

Favorite easy-to-grow annuals include cosmos (top right), which thrive in dry soil under warm weather conditions. Feathery foliage and varying heights make cosmos ideal fillers or backdrop plants in borders; these cheerful flowers also last long after cutting. Morning glories (middle right) are vines that will grow rapidly up a post or arbor and will spread into an effective screen. Marigolds (bottom right), characterized by gay, pungent blooms, also grow easily from seed. A mid-season shearing will extend their blooming period.

See the Plant Lists at the back of the book for a list of low-maintenance annuals.

Synonymous with summer, sunflowers nod beside a cottage door (opposite). Sunflowers make wonderful screens and hedges in a country garden but are equally effective as solitary sentinels. Enjoyed as cut flowers and for their tasty seeds, these open-faced annuals ~ considered weeds by some ~ climb to differing heights and may produce single or double flowers. Among the most striking varieties are the 'Italian White' and the golden 'Teddy Bear,' with its pom-pom head. Most are very adaptable, even to poor soil and dry conditions.

The Satisfaction of Vegetables & Herbs

As the bounty of a garden, vegetables and herbs offer a satisfying combination of sustenance and decoration. Despite their diverse characteristics, they are generally easy and enjoyable to grow and intermix well ~ with each other and with other kinds of plants. Even a small plot or container may be planted to both beautify the garden and fill the family larder. In fact, the whole process of preparing the proper soil "recipe," making compost as a sort of soil "starter," and concocting a tempting array of plants relates vegetable and herb gardening to the creative process of cooking.

Vegetables and many herbs are classified as edible herbaceous plants. As fleshy seed-bearers, vegetables such as tomatoes, squashes, eggplants, peppers, and corn are also termed "fruits." Other vegetables are distinguished by edible leaves (spinach and lettuce), flower buds (broccoli and artichokes), stalks (celery), pods (peas and beans), bulbs (onions), or tubers (potatoes), or a combination of two or more of these characteristics.

Most vegetables are grown as annuals from seeds,

Providing height and texture for a community garden in a city, luxuriant pole beans smother their supports (opposite). Prolific plants, they can climb from 5 to 8 feet tall. Piled in a colander, pear-shaped tomatoes (above) glisten after a good rinsing.

These "love apples" were once thought to be a dangerous aphrodisiac. It was Thomas Jefferson, an avid horticulturalist and a gourmet, who first promoted tomatoes as table food in America.

Vegetables, herbs, and flowers flourish in orderly raised beds (opposite). With such plots, the soil is easily amended and warms up faster in spring, and plants are better protected from foot traffic and mowers. Simple to grow, Swiss and ruby chard (above left) coexist happily with cosmos. Chard leaves, which taste like mild spinach when cooked, will tolerate a hard frost. A white winter squash (above right) shows its head above a summer zucchini plant.

but some, among them rhubarb and asparagus, are perennials; garlic and onions, in turn, grow from bulbs. In the case of potatoes, the actual potato tuber is cut up and planted, so that the "eyes," or buds, sprout into new specimens.

Many different approaches are taken in planting vegetable plots. Some gardeners plan crops quite scientifically for maximum harvests, preparing nutrient-rich soil and calculating frost-free planting dates. A traditional layout of straight rows allows easy access to plants, but free-form compositions also work well and can suit the casual look of a country garden. In either case, grouping vegetables according to growing season ~ tomatoes, Swiss chard, and cucumbers are long-season crops, for example, while peas, carrots, lettuce, and radishes have a short growing span ~ is recommended. It is also a smart idea

GARDENING THE ORGANIC WAY

Relying on natural products rather than man-made fertilizers and pesticides, organic gardening provides a welcome alternative to those who wish to nurture their plants without using chemicals in the process. While chemical fertilizers and pesticides can produce impressive results, often prolonging plant life, they are known to disturb the delicate balance of the soil composition, and their safety is still under debate. Moreover, they can significantly alter the taste and color of produce. Organic gardening, by contrast, will produce delicious fruits and vegetables without danger to the people who eat them, or to the environment where they are grown. It all starts with composting, a method of augmenting the soil with natural nutrients. Compost, literally a composition or mixture of decaying organic matter, may be prepared from a vast array of ingredients. These can include natural waste materials from your garden such as grass, weeds, leaves, peat moss, and pine needles, as well as food scraps from your kitchen ~ tea leaves, fish (not meat) scraps, lobster shells, and potato skins, for example, are particularly effective. Excepting cat and dog wastes, animal manure, including bat guano, tremendously.

There are various recipes for achieving the "fully cooked" dark, sweet-smelling compost that gardeners prize. The most reliable involve layering plant matter, nitrogen stimulators (manure or bone meal) to speed decomposition, minerals (ground limestone or phosphate), and rich soil or old compost as a starter.

For compost to decay, it needs heat, air, and moisture, so it is best to find a well-ventilated spot, with access to a hose, to start your pile. The material will decay on its own if you leave it long enough, but turning it every couple of weeks with a shovel or pitch fork will hasten the process. (Compost heaps covered with plastic or contained in a bin do not require turning.) Actually generating heat as it decomposes, the pile of refuse will "cook," eventually breaking down into a rich, textured mixture that can be used for mulch and for amending soil. Compost will also help add acid to alkaline soils. Every gardener benefits from testing soil for pH and mineral content; a local Cooperative Extension Service can provide advice on how to do a complete soil test.

Pest control without the aid of toxic chemical pesticides is another major thrust of organic gardening. Ladybugs, praying mantises, and lacewings are terrific consumers of such destructive insects as aphids, mealy bugs, and grasshoppers; they will also dine on their eggs and larvae. Milky spore powder, harmless to humans and beneficial insects, kills Japanese beetle grubs and the larvae of tomato hornworms and gypsy moths. Paper collars will keep cutworms at bay, and a pan of beer placed in a garden will help to immobilize slugs. Other non-intrusive options include hand-picking harmful insects from plants, or spraying them off with water or a diluted biodegradable insecticidal soap.

There are many other easy ways to improve yields naturally, as well. Crop rotation, for example, will help rejuvenate soil and improve disease resistance. Planting with regard to the effect of light and the length of day is also valuable. Some vegetables, for example, will set seed only when the days are long; others do just the opposite. Adequate thinning, weeding, and mulching to

prevent competition among plants and to help retain moisture are also requisites for a productive growing season.

Closely connected to the current interest in organic gardening is the recent effort to save older varieties of vegetables, fruits, and flowers from extinction. In fact, these "heirloom" plants have become the cherished antiques of the garden world. Many are open-pollinated varieties whose seeds can be saved and used to reproduce identical plants. By contrast, hybrids, which are crosses between two different varieties or species, cannot reproduce seed true to the original plants. Hybrids can yield improved consistency, longer blooming periods and shelf life, and better disease resistance. Heirloom fruits and vegetables, on the other hand, may not keep as long as hybrids do, but they often taste better. Moreover, they offer a welcome link to the past and provide an important gene pool for breeding new plants.

A mass of chives encircles a straw bee skep (opposite). Chives are hardy, ornamental, and flavorful herbs; clump-forming, they are ideal for edging. Their flower heads are edible when they appear in late spring or early summer, before the plants set seed. Parsley (right), as decorative as it is tasty, curls next to a hand-painted sign.

to place tall plants, such as corn, where they won't steal sun from smaller neighbors. Trellises and tepees for climbing vegetables such as beans are another possibility, and can become effective "sculptures" while saving space.

As varied as vegetables, herbs include many edible and aromatic plants, both annual and perennial, that can be used fresh or dried to flavor and preserve other foods. Foliage and flowers from lavender, lemon thyme, and scented geraniums are often dried for fragrant potpourri.

A number of herbs, including nasturtiums, clove pinks, calendulas, and borage, also produce edible flowers. Anise, coriander, and caraway are frequently grown for the seasoning value of their seeds, while other culinary types like mint, sage, basil, dill, rosemary, and tarragon are cultivated for their flavorful leaves. Tansy, on the other hand, has long been used as an insect repellent and, like many herbs, for medicinal purposes.

As plants, herbs also create strong compositions in a garden; germander, santolina, and rue, for example, are traditionally sheared into hedges. Herbs are well sited near a kitchen door, where they can be easily plucked for cooking, and will also do well in containers. Many herbs spread quickly and widely, so it is important to leave plenty of space around them, particularly if cultivating large quantities for drying. Most varieties thrive on sunshine and need excellent drainage, which is why herbs are often planted in raised beds.

chapter four

HOUSE & GARDEN

Nothing refreshes the soul better than the feel of grass between the toes, or the glimpse of a sun-dappled flower bed edging a velvet green lawn. Jealously guarded are moments spent outside, where the air is sweet and the trees all-embracing. The pleasures of being outdoors, in fact, are so great that many people are designing their homes in a way that makes it possible to enjoy the benefits of nature year-round, and that encourages maximum enjoyment of their gardens.

One logical way to bring family and guests outdoors, of course, is to entertain in the open air; even the simplest meal becomes a special occasion under the sun or stars. A porch, patio, or deck will also link house to garden while providing extra living space. By contrast, sun rooms and greenhouses bring the outdoors in, offering the opportunity to nurture plants that could not survive in the garden during cold winter months. Paths and steps are still other devices for extending the garden in all directions. And, when spruced up and incorporated into the overall landscape design, even utilitarian outbuildings such as potting sheds or rabbit hutches become design elements that can help tie house and garden together.

Entertaining, Country Living Style

Weather permitting, most people probably prefer to be outdoors rather than indoors. Very little is more liberating and refreshing than walking barefoot in the grass, listening to birds sing, and smelling the flowers – or sitting down to an open-air meal on a balmy summer evening.

It comes as no surprise, then, that many country gardeners enjoy entertaining outside, an undertaking that is sensual by nature. Their guests take visual pleasure in the careful mix of color and texture inherent in a beautiful garden; they listen for the sound of water trickling from a fountain or the pleasing tinkle of wind chimes; they breathe in the soothing fragrances of warm earth and damp grass. Even the sense of taste benefits from fresh air, as appetites are whetted and taste buds sharpened.

Barbecues and picnics, afternoon teas and lemonade parties, casual cocktails and elegant soirees: All are more memorable when the setting includes sunshine or moonlight. And just as the celebrations in a country garden can vary widely, so can the decorations and furnishings. Table settings might be improvised with

An elegant outdoor supper setting (opposite) gains romance from an abundance of Battenburg-style lace. A stone fireplace warms this patio on cool evenings, extending the season for outdoor entertaining well into autumn. Festive table decorations (above) show an imaginative eye at work. Recycled containers for casual flower arrangements include vintage milk bottles tucked inside their carrying case. A candle stands at the ready, should an afternoon get-together carry over into evening.

a few festive paper plates and napkins along with a jar of wildflowers for a centerpiece. Or, they might be made decidedly elegant, carefully orchestrated with fine china, crystal, linens, and silver candlesticks. Indeed, there is nothing wrong with bringing formal tableware outdoors for a special occasion; the same is true of dining furniture itself, which can migrate outside for a party, to be easily returned to the house when the last guest has left.

The "portable" aspect of outdoor entertaining, in fact, is one of its greatest advantages, because there is so much room for flexibility. Almost any area ~ be it a small patch of backyard grass, a spacious terrace, a deck or porch, or a waterside dock ~ is transformed with the addition of a few tables and chairs, and some appetizing food and drink. The meal doesn't have to be fancy ~ bread, fruit, and a bottle of wine are enough to create a real celebration if the spirit is right.

If the party is a daytime event, it is important to provide some shade for guests; setting up tables under umbrellas or leafy trees, or in a vine-draped pergola, will do just fine. For nighttime gatherings, soft lighting is a requisite. Candles, kerosene lanterns, and oil lamps are all traditional favorites for evening parties, as are bag lights ~ small paper sacks weighted with sand and fitted with votive candles.

Enhanced by a fine view and the fragrance of surrounding pines, a cabin porch (opposite left) serves as an outdoor dining area during warm weather. Thanks to the protective roof, even a steady rain doesn't drive guests inside. Peeled-log furniture fits the rustic setting perfectly, as do the Native American textiles. A generous front lawn (opposite right) doubles as a family picnic ground. A bucket of peppers and a container of flowers serve as colorful centerpieces. In the shade of a giant oak (above), a relaxed yet elegant summer setting was created with stoneware dishes and fine glassware. The table was fashioned from a millstone set atop a sturdy base; bright cushions are perky accents on the fold-away deck chairs.

Patios & Decks ~ Bridges to the Garden

Nothing encourages spending time outdoors quite so much as a deck or patio. Offering convenient access to the house, both types of exterior "rooms" are lovely places for dining and entertaining, reading and relaxing, or just enjoying the ambience of the garden close at hand. Patios and decks each have their own virtues and advantages, but if well designed, either will blend with its surroundings, offering sunny exposure and cooling shade, protection from wind, and attractive views.

Usually situated adjacent to the house, patios become inviting outdoor living areas with the easy addition of a few potted plants and some comfortable furnishings. These flat, open spaces are essentially defined by their surface materials ~ any of several types of cool, carefree masonry pavers.

Among the traditional patio materials is brick, which lends itself to a variety of patterns, such as running bond, basketweave, and herringbone. Rough-textured "antique" brick will provide a nonskid surface without a raw, "new" look. Flagstone, which includes slate, limestone, and granite, is another possibility but tends to be more costly, since the stone pavers should

Designed with entertaining in mind, a new deck added to a recently restored turn-of-the-century hunting lodge (above and opposite) nearly doubles the living space. Peeled-log railings and rough-hewn floorboards accent the dwelling's rustic charm, while an ivy-trimmed bridge spanning the stream in front serves as a grand entrance. Oversize candles tucked into planters make a dramatic lighting scheme.

be mortared atop a concrete slab to achieve a flat surface, whereas brick can be laid in sand. Concrete squares or rounds set in sand or mortar also make a handsome patio surface, especially when interplanted with creeping thyme, camomile, moss, or Corsican mint. Other good choices for a country look include cobblestones and fieldstones, as well as pebble and stone mosaics.

Wooden decks differ from patios in that they are raised structures and might extend from a house at any level. Decks work well for uneven terrain, as they may be cantilevered above rocky outcroppings or steep hillsides. They can also be shaped conveniently around trees and shrubs. When raised up high, they are great for taking in views. Decks are also good additions around a pool; the smooth wooden flooring is easy on bare feet, since it does not retain heat the way a masonry surface does.

Just as a well-designed patio complements the surrounding landscape, a harmoniously styled deck functions as a natural extension of the dwelling it serves. This is particularly true as the wood framing turns a silvery gray or, thanks to a well-chosen stain, takes on a hue that matches the house. Recommended decking materials include naturally rot-resistant woods such as redwood, cedar, and cypress. If less expensive pine, spruce, or fir is used, the deck should be treated with a preservative. A wooden deck coated with a penetrating stain containing a water repellent will be easier to maintain than a deck finished with paint.

Even small areas like this flagstone patio (opposite) still provide plenty of space for outdoor relaxing. Practical as well as pretty, the paved surface offers easy access to an adjacent herb garden. Wooden washtubs and firkins filled with fire-engine-red geraniums add splashes of color, while low-growing shrubs and herbs create a soft edging.

SMOOTHING THE TRANSITION

A patio built from materials that harmonize with the house it adjoins is sure to have a natural look. A flagstone surface (top), for example, blends especially well with the fieldstone-and-clapboard house, even though the patio was added some 150 years after the 200-year-old dwelling was built. The lush ground cover provides texture and softens the borders.

The brick patio (bottom), in turn, functions as a natural extension of the brick floor inside the house it serves. Generous windows and French doors further link the indoor space with the garden and yard just beyond.

A lakeside deck (above), shaded naturally by tall trees, takes advantage of the appealing view. Container plants bring a garden feeling to this outdoor "room." Outside a converted barn (right), a simple platform-style deck serves as a stage for a collection of antique garden ornaments and rustic furniture; sliding glass doors permit easy access to the house.

Serene Porches

Sitting on the front porch and enjoying a gentle summer breeze is a country pleasure of the purest sort. Even with the rain falling in a soft, steady drizzle, the porch is the place to be, protected from the elements yet still close to nature. Here, long, lazy afternoons are savored, books read, catnaps taken, and gossip exchanged.

Long valued for both its practical and aesthetic attributes, the American porch owes its origins to a number of different sources. The idea of such a cool, outdoor room was brought to the Colonies by way of the West Indies as early as about 1700, and many houses built in the South after that time featured a porch or gallery - both upstairs and down - to capture cooling breezes and maximize cross ventilation.

Another type of porch was the Flemish *stoep*, or stoop, a small sheltered area common to houses built here by Flemish settlers in the late eighteenth and early nineteenth centuries. Located just outside the front entry, the stoop was often furnished with a pair of benches and offered a place for callers to wait, out of the snow and rain.

Still another American porch type, the classical portico, an outgrowth of the Greek Revival movement, was popular from about 1820 to 1840. Usually found at the entry or side of a house, an elegant partico lent a

The pretty porch on an 1856 dwelling (opposite) features wicker furnishings and gingerbread trim; gray deck paint protects the well-trodden floor. An appealing back porch (above) was created when a wooden platform and open roof trellis were built onto a cottage. The simple addition has greatly extended the living space of the small house.

stately air to new houses of the period, as well as to the many Colonial dwellings then being remodeled to suit changing architectural fashions.

By the mid-nineteenth century, when fresh air was considered essential to good health, the porch had become a full-fledged outdoor room. Sometimes, multiple porches protruding at all angles adorned a house, with screened-in areas on the upper floors used for sleeping. Ornate brackets, bargeboards (decorative trim covering the rafter ends under a gabled roof), and scrollwork were the distinguishing features of these elaborate Victorian confections – the products of revolutionary steam-powered sawmills and new nail-making plants that could turn out fancy fretwork swiftly and inexpensively.

Furnished with comfortable rockers, wicker settees, or romantic swings, Victorian porches provided a welcome link between house and garden, offering shelter as well as air and light – enough air and light, in fact, for vines and potted flowers to flourish.

With today's emphasis on entertaining at home, porches are once again appreciated for all the pleasure they can give. Old-time swings and wicker furnishings are still available to enhance a vintage look. Be it a narrow wraparound veranda, a large screened-in room, or a tiny side portico with space for a single rocker, a porch makes it possible to enjoy outdoor living and still be protected from gusts of wind or sudden showers.

A Victorian-style porch swing brings an old-time look to a relatively new house (opposite left). Here, easy-care potted geraniums appear on steps, in corners, and hanging in baskets. On the front porch of a cottage (opposite right), cut flowers, a folk-art birdhouse, and a primitive portrait make an imaginative still life. A porch entry (right), in turn, displays a washtub and crates of petunias, along with a hanging fuchsia. Here, period details include the whimsical Victorian fretwork decorating the roof overhang and the screened door. The porch of a 1923 mountain camp built in upstate New York (overleaf) offers plenty of seating options. Rough-hewn timber posts and mix-and-match wicker and rattan furniture brand it an Adirondack classic.

CLIMBING VINES

Welcome additions to a country porch, vines are superb for bringing texture and color to small areas and for creating shade and promoting a general feeling of coolness.

This versatile family of long-stemmed plants comprises a surprising range of types: Vines may be annual or perennial, deciduous or evergreen, herbaceous or woody, sun- or shade-loving. Many produce showy flowers and striking autumn foliage, as well as vegetables, fruit, and seed pods.

For all their variety, however, vines do share at least one common attribute: their ability to climb. This is done in several ways. Some vines send out clinging tendrils, while others hold on with twining stems or winding leafstalks called petioles; still others grip with tiny sticky adhesive discs or with aerial rootlets.

Because different species have different climbing methods, vines need to be matched to their supports with care. Ivies, climbing hydrangeas, and creepers, for instance, are very effective covering rough brick or stone pillars and walls. Their rootlets or discs, on the other hand, are apt to cause wooden shingles and siding to heave and can damage wooden trellises. Ivies are a poor choice for crumbling masonry, because the greenery can force its way into the joints and weaken them. Twining vines, such as clematis, five-leaf akebias, and silver fleece, grow best on open or lattice supports, although some, like wisteria and Hall's honeysuckle, may overwhelm their supports if they are allowed.

For more information on vines, see the Plant Lists at the back of the book.

Lush grapevines create a lacy curtain for a rustic porch (right). Grapevines attach themselves to supports with tendrils, but most need tying as well. Making an excellent screen, the large toothed leaves turn vivid red in autumn; when they fall, they expose an intriguing tangle of woody stems.

A weathered look predominates on the porch of a wilderness cabin (opposite), where potted petunias, asparagus ferns, lobelias, geraniums, and a wreath of flax contribute color. Board-and-batten siding typical of American houses built in the second half of the nineteenth century is the backdrop for a cozy porch (right) stocked with country finds: stoneware, textiles, toleware, and baskets. The paint on the recycled bench, formerly a church pew, has faded from red to soft rose. In the background, dried herbs and flowers hang from an elevator door salvaged from an old industrial building. The weather-resistant, painted floorcloth works well in this outdoor setting.

Sun-Filled Garden Rooms

There is no better way to bring the pleasures of gardening indoors than with a sunny, glass-enclosed room filled with plants. A garden room not only helps brighten a house that might otherwise be dark, but also provides hospitable surroundings for a changing display of flowers, herbs, and fruits that would not survive outside in cold weather. With the right amount of warmth and light, seeds can be started, plants nurtured, and spirits lifted, even in the dead of winter.

Bricks make practical floor pavers for a cheerful sun room (opposite). Located just off the kitchen, the space serves as both a breakfast room and a potting area. In a prefabricated conservatory (above), a broad expanse of glass frames the room's stunning vista. A spacious garden room (overleaf) was designed with a transparent corrugated roof for maximum sunshine.

Almost any type of garden room increases the range of possible plants ~ everything from familiar standbys like philodendrons to small trees and exotic tropical orchids ~ that can be cultivated inside. Serious gardeners might consider a traditional greenhouse, built right onto the house for economy and convenience. Fitted with double-insulated glass and a waterproof brick or stone floor, a greenhouse sustains a practical plant-growing environment, where light, temperature, and humidity can be carefully controlled.

However ideal for plants, a greenhouse can be uncomfortably warm and damp for people. If the primary purpose of a garden room is to open up a house with light, a casual solarium, or sun room, is a good alternative. A solarium might be nothing more than a room with lots of windows or a porch enclosed with thermal glass, as long as there is plenty of sunshine to keep potted plants healthy. With a few appealing furnishings ~ wicker is

perfect for evoking warm summer days - a solarium is an ideal spot for reading, or simply musing, and an equally attractive place for entertaining guests.

Another possibility for a garden room is a conservatory, a cross between the plant-perfect greenhouse and the people-friendly sun room. Descended from the elaborate plant-filled structures popular in Victorian times, today's conservatories shelter plants without sacrificing comfort. Numerous windows allow cooling cross ventilation, and there is plenty of space for eye-catching arrangements of potted plants.

French doors open onto a small greenhouse (opposite top) built from a kit. Within its warm, moist confines, ferns and geraniums flourish, and the natural light from the glass-enclosed addition floods the adjacent dining room year-round. The comfortable sun room (opposite bottom) was remodeled from a seldom-used side porch and is now a favorite spot for reading, entertaining, and starting seedlings; it also serves as a painting studio. An elegant garden room (right) was created when a 1908 conservatory was dismantled and moved to a new site. In warm weather, the doors, windows, and transoms are opened to catch breezes. Set directly on the ground, the weathered brick floor pavers frame small garden beds, which benefit from the extended growing season the sunny room makes possible.

Beckoning Paths

Just as Shakespeare's primrose path led to dalliance, so, perhaps, do the best country walkways. A good path entices visitors into a garden, and also encourages them to spend time enjoying the surroundings firsthand.

Yet a walkway can do even more for a country garden: It can provide a sense of movement ~ a suggestion of somewhere to go ~ especially when punctuated by a bench or sculpture that offers a point of focus. Depending on its contours and materials, a path also accentuates the feeling established by the plantings in a garden or yard. A straight walk paved in neat flagstone squares would work well in a formal layout of symmetrical hedges and flower beds, for instance, while a meandering path of clam shells might suit a casual seaside garden where straight lines have no place.

Bark chips and autumn leaves make a textured carpet for a privet-bordered allée (above left), where the shrub branches meet overhead to form a living tunnel. A small yard (above right) gains interest from two different pathways ~ one of randomly placed stones, the other of bricks laid end-to-end. Intersecting paths delineate herb and perennial beds (opposite), while the loose gravel surface keeps the look casual.

At their most basic, paths are practical, providing distinct links between different areas of a yard and offering access to the house, garage, and other buildings found on a property. Within a garden, they can function as "hallways," dividing an area into "rooms" for different plantings ~ roses, herbs, or flowering bulbs, perhaps ~ while offering easy access to plant beds. Paths may also be used to draw visitors, and their

attention, away from a potential eyesore such as a utility shed or a compost heap.

In designing a garden path, materials are key to establishing a distinctive character. Providing welcome texture and durability, brick, cobblestone, and fieldstone all make good surfaces. Flagstone, which can be rough-cut in random shapes or laid in uniform pavers, is also a smart choice.

Because of its natural, informal look, wood ~ including planks and hardwood rounds ~ also works particularly well in a country garden. Less permanent than stone and brick, however, wood is subject to decay and is best treated with a preservative.

Loose materials such as wood chips, pine needles, and gravel can also look just right. They not only provide good drainage but are generally inexpensive and easy to put down. Grass also has a lovely appearance that links a path naturally to the rest of a yard, but it does need regular mowing and weeding.

FRAGRANT BORDER PLANTS

One of the delights of walking along a garden path comes from breathing in the scent of flowers and foliage as you brush by. Some gardeners, in fact, choose border plants specifically with perfume in mind. Among the possibilities, of course, are flowers, including particularly pleasant-smelling perennials such as English primrose, sweet violet, and the poet's narcissus, as well as fragrant annuals like old-fashioned single petunia and Drummond phlox.

Other scented plants, however, also work well for walkways. You might consider cultivating a hedge of boxwood or santolina, for example. Unusual varieties of herbs such as chocolate mint, catmint, caraway, and lemon thyme and old favorites like the nasturtiums 'Golden Gleam' and 'Fiery Festival' can be very effective ribboning a pathway or creeping out of the cracks between pavers. Fine-leafed bush basil can be massed very effectively, while rosemary trims into a marvelous hedge in temperate climates.

Whatever the choice of plants, it is important to consider how the fragrances will mix. Don't try to put too many varieties together, and avoid using a plant whose perfume may overwhelm the scent of others. One good way to plant is to stagger blooming times, so that different fragrances will prevail in different seasons.

For a list of plants recommended for scented borders, see the Plant Lists at back of the book.

Pine-bark chips form tidy pathways (opposite) in a garden featuring raised beds of vegetables, herbs, and flowers. Timbers salvaged from an old bridge were combined with loose chips to make a distinctive walkway (right). Clematis and roses add height to the scene, as do the Monterey pines, which double as a wind screen.

A Step at a Time

Old or new, curved or straight, an outdoor staircase welcomes visitors and helps set the tone in a country garden. Steps can stage an intriguing entrance, enticing callers to climb or descend them to see what lies beyond. They might lead the way to a noteworthy spot, such as a sheltered nook or commanding view, and also function well as links between different outdoor areas.

Even a concrete staircase (opposite) can enhance the look of a country garden. Baskets of snapdragons and Spanish moss accent every second step, adding to the sense of welcome. An ordinary wooden staircase (above) was transformed with green paint; filled with petunias and phlox, a collection of watering cans marches up the treads and reinforces the garden theme.

Steps also incorporate architectural elements and may become effective showcases for a display of favorite collectibles or potted plants.

An old staircase rejuvenated with stain or paint, or spruced up with pots of flowers strategically set on the treads, can prove more pleasing than a newly constructed, pristine flight of steps. Staircases may contain built-in planters and offer additional seating on retaining or side walls.

When made from thoughtfully chosen materials, steps also provide interesting texture and focal points in a garden. The possibilities range from brick and bluestone to wood chips and rustic-looking logs. Banked with plants or softened with ground cover, a staircase fashioned from any of these natural surfaces will send a message of rustic charm.

Wisteria wraps its way through the railing of a wooden staircase (opposite), where a collection of garden ornaments forms a welcoming committee. Wide steps (above) become an extra seating area. Old millstones make handsome stairs for a path outside a renovated mill house (near right). Naturalistic rock steps are a fitting approach to a rustic cabin (far right).

Building on the Back Forty

Although storage space is often treated as an afterthought, outbuildings for holding seeds, compost, pots, tools, and all the other accoutrements associated with gardening are important to a successful growing season. And while sometimes neglected, such useful structures as barns and sheds have the potential to add an extra dimension to a garden's overall design.

Beyond their role as storehouses, outbuildings can have a charm of their own and therefore deserve as much attention as the rest of the garden. An existing structure that has gone unnoticed for years can be made presentable with surprising ease. Paint – in colors that complement those of the main house, perhaps – will spruce up a featureless shed; treated to trompe l'oeil decoration, an outbuilding might even become a design focus, adding an element of welcome surprise to a yard and offering balance to the house.

Any outbuilding, old or new, can also be integrated into a yard with the help of plantings. Wall trellises, for example, will provide support for vines, espalier fruit trees, or carefree climbing roses that help camouflage unattractive structures or building materials that may appear too new to blend in well with their surroundings. Shrubs, tall-growing flowers such as hollyhocks and sunflowers, and other foundation plantings further soften edges with color and texture.

Fortunately, it's never too late to add an outbuilding. Perhaps most desirable of all are those that serve more than one purpose. A storage shed that doubles as a potting room is welcome indeed. A thoughtfully designed pool house, in turn, will keep cleaning equipment and chemicals out of harm's way while offering a place for guests to change or to congregate during a sudden summer shower.

A raised flower bed, complete with a wagon of petunias, coleus, and marigolds (above), helps a storage shed (opposite) blend with its surroundings. Sheathed with shingles and board-and-batten siding, the little building has a simple charm well suited to a country garden.

BERRETT
MASTER BUILDER

Fitting comfortably into the surrounding cornfield, a new pool house (left) looks as though it has been in place for years. The building provides useful storage for pool furniture and supplies, along with sleeping quarters for guests. No longer housing livestock, an early nineteenth-century barn (above) on a New England farm has found new life as home office space. Morning glories and moonflowers climb up the sides.

chapter five

THE WELL-FURNISHED GARDEN

Practical as well as attractive, well-chosen outdoor furnishings supply the finishing touches to a yard or garden. In a country garden, structural elements such as gates, fences, and trellises are rarely strictly utilitarian, but often double as decorative features that can complete an overall look. A rustic split-rail fence, for instance, may ensure privacy and define a garden plot, but it might also help emphasize a carefree country feeling already established by the plantings.

A one-of-a-kind gate, in turn, will beckon the curious to enter a garden, while well-placed seating will invite them to relax and stay a while. As movable gardens, plant-filled containers supply their own flourishes to decks, patios, steps, and walkways. Even the smallest garden ornaments, along with birdhouses and birdbaths, play an important role, working as points of interest in a landscape while expressing the personal style of the gardeners who have chosen them.

At the Garden Gate

The phrase "Meet me at the garden gate" has always conveyed the thrill of romance. One glance at a gate topped by a pretty trellis or graced with a filigree of fine wrought iron hints that something intriguing lies beyond.

Whether sending a message of welcome or reinforcing privacy, a gate offers the opportunity to make a statement about a garden. An iron gate flanked by a brick wall might establish entry to a rather formal yard, for example, while one of weathered pickets is more likely to promise the casual tangle of a cottage garden.

A painted wooden gate (opposite) conveys an all-American greeting and proves there is room for originality in a traditional setting. A latticework gate (above) matches the surrounding fence, while scroll brackets and urns add decorative interest to this garden entry.

A gate that looks at home in a country garden can, in fact, be chosen from a surprising range of possibilities. Among the most familiar types are the traditional picket and post-and-rail styles, but in the right place, a rustic gate made of knobby branches or even a Gothic or classic Chippendale design can be successful.

Whatever its style, a gate should respect the look of the house and garden it serves. Logically, then, its design and materials depend on its immediate surroundings. In many cases, a gate simply echoes the style of fence or wall where it is located. There doesn't always have to be an exact match, however; a white latticework gate set in a hedge, for instance, makes an effective entry, calling attention to itself through a deliberate contrast of color and materials.

The profile of a picket gate (left) flatters the curving design of the trellis overhead. Flanked by a border of ornamental perennials and herbs, the gate makes an inviting entry through a privet hedge. Sweet autumn clematis climbs over the arch.

A weathered popsicle-stick gate (top right) features a wire-mesh underguard designed to keep hungry varmints out of the garden. In a clever design, big fish gobbles little fish (center right). With a simpler approach, rough pine and wide-gauge wire mesh make a country gate for a vegetable garden (bottom right). The wooden cutouts suggest where the resident gardener keeps her heart.

The shape of the gate is also a consideration. A simple rectangle is only one possibility; for added interest, a gate might dip or curve at the top, or take the profile of a familiar object, such as the American flag. And when crowned with a bonnet or trellis, a gate becomes a charming support for climbing vines and roses.

A well-designed gate not only complements its surroundings but also functions well. It should open and close smoothly, of course, and be wide enough to admit expected traffic, which might include equipment like lawnmowers and tractors as well as people. Ideally, a gate should measure no more than four feet in width; anything larger tends to sag. Double gates, braced to prevent dragging, can accommodate larger openings.

Stone and brick work well for gateposts, but wood posts should be sunk into the ground at a depth at least one third of their length. It is a good idea to coat metal latches or hinges with a weather-resistant protector, even if they are to be painted.

Fences – Plain & Fancy

An integral part of the American landscape, fences serve a multitude of purposes, both practical and decorative. Used to create privacy, to establish security, and to mark property lines, they help enclose a garden or yard and work to define cultivated areas within. Fences also function as attractive backdrops for plantings and offer support to low-growing shrubs as well as to vines and climbing roses.

Natural additions to country gardens, fences have a longstanding heritage in America. Indeed, they were once the law of the land; the town fathers of Williamsburg, Virginia, founded in 1705, required that houses be surrounded by a fence or wall to keep out livestock, which roamed freely in the streets.

Not surprisingly, most of the familiar regional fence types that developed throughout the country were born of practicality. The low stone walls that still thread their way through rural New England, for example, were repositories for the countless rocks that heaved up naturally and had to be hand-picked from the land before planting could begin.

In Southern regions, on the other hand, farmers tended to favor zigzag split-rail fences, also known as worm or snake fences. Fashioned from local hardwoods such as oak, ash, and walnut, zigzag fences required no nails and could be assembled with a single tool: the axe. Although these enclosures used an enormous amount of wood, a farmer could split as many as a hundred rails

Shasta daisies, lythrum, and bee balm peek through a fence with arrowhead pickets painted white to match the house trim (opposite). The proliferation of mechanized sawmills after the Revolutionary War helped the wooden picket fence take hold as one of America's most popular types. A distinctive fence (above) shows the possibility for imaginative design; the tops of the pales are shaped like whimsical quails.

GOOD FENCES....

Country fences need be neither new nor perfect: Indeed, if the rails are out of plumb or the gate leans a bit to one side, the effect can be all the more charming. A long-lasting wooden fence, however, always depends on good materials. The best choices for ground posts are decay-resistant heartwoods – cedar, cypress, and redwood – or pressure-treated lumber (woods treated with CCA – chromated copper arsenate – are generally recommended over other types). Pressure-treated lumber, which is usually pine, is not as strong as the heartwoods, but it is less expensive and actually more impervious to rot and insects. It works well for secondary parts of a fence, such as the pickets, boards, and rails.

An applied finish may also prolong the life of a fence. Paint is a good protector; so are stains, especially those containing fungicides and water-repellents. Clear preservatives are also available; these maintain the look of natural wood, yet minimize mildew and warping.

in a day. An alternative to the zigzag type was the post-and-rail fence, which followed a straight line; it needed far less wood and was more economical to build.

With their natural look, such traditional fences are very appropriate for country gardens; in addition to zigzag and post-and-rail designs, peeled-pole, wattle (poles interlaced with slender reeds or branches), and board fences are also good choices. The picket fence, too, is a versatile favorite, offering limitless possibilities for varying the designs of the pales and posts.

No matter what their type, most fences benefit from judicious planting designed to soften their lines. Picket fences, for instance, look charming entwined with morning glories, or with the faces of sunflowers peeking through the pales. Even a chain-link fence can be "countrified" with a thick growth of evergreen ivy.

Flexible branches and bits of string were used to make a rustic wattle fence (opposite), which is perfectly suited to the easygoing demeanor of the resident "scarecrow." A weathered picket fence (right), entwined with red roses, provides a backdrop for an old-fashioned mix of larkspurs, pink and white phlox, and red amaryllis.

Romantic Trellises & Arbors

Who can resist a romantic rose-covered arbor or a trellis laced with honeysuckle? These versatile forms of garden architecture have long appealed to country gardeners for their ability to spark interest in even the smallest of outdoor areas. Inviting and pretty, arbors and trellises offer an attractive refuge in which to contemplate verdant surroundings. Perhaps most importantly, they provide supports for training an endlessly interesting array of plants, from deciduous and evergreen vines to climbing roses. The real magic happens when these plants take over. Then they become a natural extension of their supports, while they assume an architectural quality all their own.

Made of latticework panels, trellises can be flat or three-dimensional and are readily tailored to suit a specific site. They might screen a window or porch, or be set slightly apart from a wall or roof to prevent climbing plants from damaging shingles, clapboards, or brick. These simple structural elements, which were extremely popular in American gardens throughout the eighteenth and early nineteenth centuries, also take easily to decorative shapes that make their own contribution to a landscape.

Arbors go one step further than trellises by supporting plants while forming actual enclosures; often arched, they might serve as a little shelter for a bench,

An arbor swathed in roses (above) tempts visitors to pass through. Gardeners have long turned to bowers such as this to create a transition from one garden area to another. Near the seashore, an arbor-topped gate (opposite) frames a view of a shingled building, where trellises climbing the walls and roof support moisture-loving climbers. Privet is trained over the arch, while rambling roses scramble across the roof on frames that surround the dormers.

perhaps, or as a gateway. Sometimes, to create the illusion of extra space, an arbor may be placed at the extreme end of a yard, hinting that something more lies beyond. But a plant-covered arbor ~ rustic branches draped with grape vines, or white lattice tangled in roses ~ serves equally well as a garden centerpiece. For drama, a series of arbors may be extended into a tunnel-like gallery, or designed as a pergola, which is a colonnade with a flat openwork roof that can be interwoven with plants that offer shade.

Although ready-made trellises and arbors are easy to purchase, homemade versions are just as viable; the more rustic and natural their appearance, in fact, the better they fit into a country garden. Actual branches might be fashioned into an eccentric yet rustic design, while pressure-treated lumber suits a simple post-and-beam design.

Regardless of their form, arbors and trellises do need maintenance. A well-constructed frame has a life span of about twenty years and requires regular re-painting, re-staining, and sometimes rebuilding.

Honeysuckle and morning glory vines wrap their way around a hillside arbor (opposite), creating a natural picture window. Properly planted, vines like these require little maintenance beyond occasional pruning. Young rose plants work their way up a trellised arbor in a yard where a breathtaking display of bluebonnets and Indian paintbrush carpets the ground (above). Trellis panels woven with sweet peas form living curtains for cottage windows (right).

Wisteria and a ground-cover of lavender add fragrance to this corner of a country garden. Supper beneath a canopy of grapevines is a serene affair in a rustic pergola (overleaf). This traditional garden structure, outside a nineteenth-century sea captain's cottage, was fashioned from bark-covered logs. Requiring minimum upkeep, the native grapevines bear an abundance of fruit every year.

An extravagant spill of blushing 'New Dawn' roses blooms on a trellised gateway (left). This apple-scented variety, which may grow up to ten feet in one year, was introduced in 1930. It is the world's first patented rose.

CLIMBING ROSES

Nothing looks more romantic in a country garden than an arbor or trellis lush with sprays of climbing roses. These beautiful and versatile plants are essentially shrubs with extra-long canes, or branches, and fall into several categories.

Among the favorite climbing roses are those known as "large-flowered climbers." They are characterized by clusters of medium- to large-size blossoms; some may flower only once, while others are repeat bloomers. Another type, known as "ramblers," has clusters of small flowers and sends out flexible canes that are easily trained on arbors and fences. "Hybrid Wichuraiana climbers," another category of climber, are bred from a species rose known for its long trailing canes. The star of this type is 'New Dawn,' which bears masses of fragrant, pale pink, semi-double blooms in June, with a good recurrence thereafter.

All climbing roses are shown off to best advantage on some sort of support. Because most of the roses sprout flowering shoots that need to grow horizontally, arbors, trellises, and fences make good frameworks for them. There are also climbers, however, that do better on posts, trees, and walls, so it is important to be sure that the right rose is matched to the right support.

PLANTING

Although potted plants are available from nurseries, many people buy roses through catalogs. Mail-order roses are shipped as dormant, bare-root (no soil) plants in the spring. The roots must be soaked in water up to 24 hours before planting. To train the canes without damaging them, it is best to tie them loosely to their supports with soft twine or stretchy plastic tape. A nursery can provide local guidelines for special care and feeding.

PRUNING

Different climbers have different pruning needs. The cane ends of "ramblers" should be cut back immediately after the plants flower to stimulate production of the horizontal shoots that will produce blooms the following season.

On one-time blooming "large-flowered climbers," the faded blossoms should be cut off, except on those varieties that set decorative hips. On repeat bloomers, it is best to snip back the stems to the first set of five-leaflet leaves after the flowers wither. Any extensive pruning of dead wood and weak canes on both one-time and repeat bloomers should wait until late winter. In any case, avoid over-pruning, which will detract from the natural shape that make climbers so wonderful.

For more information on climbing roses, see the Plant Lists at the back of the book.

Versatile Furniture

Whether of wicker, wood, cast iron, or stone, outdoor furniture completes the country garden setting. From the vantage point of a well-sited bench or chair, visitors can survey their surroundings and linger in comfort; even on a chilly morning, a garden seat is a fine place to start the day. Outdoor tables and companion chairs make dining al fresco a pleasure, while easy groupings of lounge chairs are ideal for soaking in the sun. And, casually slung between two trees, a comfortable hammock conveys a statement all its own, inviting passersby to wile away an afternoon in timeless comfort.

Furnishings for the country garden include designs both old and new. Many good reproductions of classics, such as the Chippendale-style bench, are available, but flea-market finds touched up with a fresh coat of paint, as well as creative improvisations ~ a board propped up on a couple of cast-off logs, for example ~ are charming and adaptable alternatives.

Furnishings in the Adirondack style can also make an effective addition to a country garden. These naturalistic pieces are often fashioned from branches and tree trunks, with knots, gnarled roots, and bark left intact for a rustic effect. Trappers and guides in the Adirondack Mountain wilderness of upstate New York perfected the type in the late nineteenth and early twentieth centuries, expanding their repertoire to include a wide range of tables, chairs, and benches.

Peeling paint only enhances the simple charm of a garden bench (above) overlooking a naturalistic swimming pool (opposite). A rope hammock atop a hill offers still another spot for outdoor relaxation. This versatile garden furnishing can easily be moved around a yard. Come winter, it is simply rolled up and stored until the following spring.

With its simple lines, the familiar Adirondack chair is thought to have originated in 1905 in the lakeside town of Westport, New York, as the work of an amateur carpenter attempting to build a comfortable seat with as few materials as possible. Distinguished by a high back, deep sloping seat, and flat board arms, this carefree wooden furnishing has proved an enduring addition to the American garden.

Lightweight and comfortable, wicker ~ a catch-all term for pieces made of woven rattan, willow, rush, reed, and cane ~ has also long had a place in garden rooms, and on porches and patios. (Although rain can damage these porous materials, the humidity inherent in conservatories is actually beneficial because it keeps wicker from drying out.) Since Victorian times, classic white, dark-green, and natural-hued wicker furnishings have contributed character and, in the most elaborate styles, a touch of whimsy, to their surroundings.

Cast-iron tables and chairs, especially those reproduced from nineteenth-century styles, are another choice. Introduced around 1840, the first cast-iron furniture was made for the outdoors, and imitated the same organic forms displayed by rustic wooden furniture. The look was perfect for the romantic, naturalistic gardens popular throughout most of the Victorian era, and it evokes a sense of nostalgia today.

Garden furniture can be a means for self-expression. Made by a contemporary folk artist in New Mexico, an unusual high-backed bench (above right) features carved-and-painted geese and gaily painted flowers. Not all furniture needs to be new or custom-made, however. Clever recycling is also effective: A 110-year-old church pew (right) now makes a charming bench for a log-cabin porch. Rustic benches can also be easily crafted from bits and pieces of salvaged lumber.

THE CHARM OF WEATHERED WOOD

Reinforcing a sense of timelessness, furniture of weathered wood has a special place in the country garden. Preferring the worn, comfortable look of such pieces, many gardeners will in fact purposely expose new wood to rain, snow, and sun in order to hasten the natural aging process.

Wood furniture left to weather outdoors year-round needs some protection, however. One good way to achieve this is by applying a water repellent, which allows wood to mellow without subjecting it to the full force of the elements. A water repellent is especially effective on furniture made of cedar, redwood, or teak, because it lets the warm colors of these handsome woods show through. (Such a finish should be applied every two years, or when rain water begins to puddle rather than bead.)

More noticeable than clear protective agents, semi-transparent, oil-based penetrating stains – containing both a fungicide and a water-repellent – will introduce color to wood while still showing off the grain. When applied to new oak or pine, these stains simulate a weathered look in short order, with little or no help from Mother Nature.

Favored by some for its dramatically rustic effect, the look of flaking paint is another option. Left outdoors for a winter or two, painted pieces will begin to peel, revealing the wood underneath.

Antique chairs and a matching table (above) display a wireworker's talent. Painted white, the metal grouping complements the pink-and-white flower garden. Separate seating areas (opposite top) make the most of an inviting yard and provide a variety of destinations for visitors. In the foreground, wicker bistro chairs surround a quilt-topped table set for a warm-weather snack of strawberries and lemonade. In the background, a teak bench offers a perfect place to indulge in a good novel. Shaded by an umbrella, the Adirondack chair collapses for easy storage and transport. A rustic wooden bench (opposite bottom left) looks as if it grew right out of the ground. Equally distinctive, the set of outdoor furniture (opposite bottom right) was inspired by the Gothic Revival designs popular from about 1840 to 1880.

ARRANGING GARDEN FURNITURE

The placement of furniture is often as important to overall garden composition as the location of the plantings, and can have a surprisingly strong effect on setting a mood and determining how an outdoor area is used. Furniture groupings shaded from the hot sun will encourage friendly gatherings, while a solitary bench nestled under a fragrant bower promises solace at the end of a long day. Outdoor furniture can also serve as garden sculpture of sorts. Strategically placed in the center of an herb garden or at a bend in a long herbaceous border, a distinctive bench or seat becomes an eye-catching design element in itself.

Site and use go hand in hand when arranging garden furniture. A flat terrace or clearing supplied with tables and comfortable chairs, for instance, is likely to become an irresistible spot for outdoor dining and entertaining, especially when there is easy access to the kitchen. On the other hand, a bench or hammock set a distance from the house will accentuate a feeling of privacy, and invite solitary pursuits such as afternoon napping. A seat tucked into an alcove screened by thick wisteria or other vines promises pleasant tranquillity as well.

Container Gardens

Plantings in a country garden are seldom confined to beds of flowers and vegetables. Nooks and crannies around a house and yard also offer spots for an endless variety of blooms, potted in everything from wooden crates to tin buckets.

Indccd, plants grown in containcrs bring a dash of wit to staircases, patios, and doorways and provide quick and easy seasonal color as well as portable fragrance. A few pots of flowers add interest to an ordinary doorstep and, placed judiciously, will help fill out a new bed where permanent plantings haven't had the chance to come into their own. Container gardening has other benefits, too: It allows just about anyone to raise plants - even apartment dwellers and thosc with a yard no biggcr than a postagc stamp.

Importantly, containers also permit gardeners to create micro-climates best suited to individual species, and to nurture plants in customized conditions. Tender, shade-loving holly ferns, for example, which need regular watering and a potting mixture rich in leaf mold, can be hard to grow in a garden, yet they can thrive in baskets filled with specially prepared soil and hung in a cool spot. In Southern regions, where even sun-loving annuals may wilt in the noonday heat, pots make it easy to move such plants as petunias, snapdragons, and lobelias into the shade whenever the temperature dictates.

Two wine crates supply happy homes for double-ruffled petunias (opposite); weathered containers such as these make ideal seed flats as well as planters. Deep-blue lobelias and white petunias tumble from a sturdy graniteware bucket (above). This versatile container is easily transported from back steps to kitchen table, where it becomes an impromptu centerpiece.

The range of containers appropriate to a country garden is limited only by the imagination. Traditional choices include terra-cotta pots, which are available in the usual round sizes and as oblong planters that look good perched on a wall or windowsill.

Urns, barrels, wooden cases, and buckets all can be planters as well. Troughs and shallow bowls make appropriate homes for miniature rock gardens, while freestanding tubs offer lovely settings for small, soothing water gardens, or for portable herb gardens, which can be conveniently placed by the kitchen door.

Whatever the choice, no container or its contents should be left untended. Temperature fluctuations, severe weather, and wind are likely to affect container-bound plants more quickly than those growing right in the ground, so care must be taken to provide pots with shelter as needed. In winter, plants left to weather outdoors benefit from a mulch of straw, and in harsh climates (those in which the thermometer dips below zero for a week or more at a stretch), they need a burlap wrapper. Ceramic and terra-cotta pots are best stored in a basement or shed, protected from the freeze-thaw cycle that causes them to crack.

A grape-festooned planter (top) holds a cascade of marigolds, while the whimsical cart (above) displays bunches of boltonias, yellow chrysanthemums, and marigolds. Soft-gray stain makes the pieces, both of cedar, look antique, but they are actually almost new. Such sturdy hand-carved planters are extremely resistant to the elements.

POTTING TIPS

An enormous variety of plants grow happily in containers. These include not only annuals and herbaceous perennials, but also bulbs, corms and tubers, and even small trees and shrubs. Climbing vines, vegetables, fruit, miniature alpines, and water-loving varieties can also be potted.

The key to success is choosing the right container. Healthy plants make their homes in pots large enough to accommodate root development, yet small enough to show off the plant in proper scale (an oversized container will dwarf its tenant). A good rule of thumb is to choose a pot that is an inch wider in diameter than the root ball. A container with at least one hole in the bottom is recommended, but if there are no holes, a layer of gravel or marble chips about an inch deep will help prevent roots from drowning.

A standard recipe for soil preparation is one part perlite or coarse builder's sand, one part peat moss or compost, and two parts good sterile potting soil. Adjust the mix accordingly for acid-loving plants, such as azaleas and hydrangeas, and for those that prefer alkaline conditions, such as clematis.

Nearly all potted annuals, perennials, trees, and shrubs require more frequent watering than plants growing right in the ground, so check often to see if the soil is dry. A weekly feeding with a liquid fertilizer is recommended for annuals; potted perennials and roses can be fed about once every three weeks. An initial high-nitrogen fertilizer feeding will promote vigorous growth of perennials and fruiting plants. This should be followed with a high-potassium liquid tomato fertilizer to encourage heavy flowering.

A variety of winsome containers serve as planters on a country terrace (left). Feathery pink astilbe fills a wooden bucket, while assorted perennials are packed into a wheelbarrow no longer suited to yard duty but perfect for showing off potted plants. When stormy weather threatens, the gay display is easily wheeled out of harm's way.

REBORN CONTAINERS

While a wide range of commercially made containers are available to gardeners, outdoor planters can be created from almost any weather-resistant object that will hold soil. Indeed, flea-market finds and recycled kitchenware often have more character than a conventional planter purchased in a store.

An old enamel roasting pan filled with posies, a hollow log overflowing with geraniums, or a galvanized tin bucket bursting with marigolds is sure to create a look of country charm. Reused containers don't have to be small: Wagons and carts are likely candidates for cargoes of plants, as are leaky rowboats and decommissioned canoes. Planters can also be used to reflect a gardener's personality or environment. Retired lobster pots, clamming baskets, and cranberry scoops might be pressed into service near the New England coast, for instance, while a wine keg makes a logical choice in California's vineyard country.

Whatever the type, every container should be thoroughly cleaned before use, because any existing algae, fertilizer deposits, or bacteria is potentially damaging to plants. A soap-and-water bath followed by a gentle rinse with diluted bleach (no more than one part bleach to nine parts water) will ready recycled containers for new tenants.

A old cast-iron school bell (left) tops a signpost where witty animal signs spell out directions to the front door of the house. Garden ornaments like the hand-carved cedar menagerie in a bed of marigolds and ageratums can be unobtrusive yet decorative (opposite left). A fool-the-eye urn of flowers (opposite right) rests atop a column carved from wood.

Whimsies & Weathervanes

Sculpture and statuary, birdhouses and birdbaths, even lampposts and signs bring personality to yards of all dimensions. Added after the body of the garden ~ its plots and bed formations ~ is established, these imaginative flourishes serve as more than mere ornament. They are the finishing touches that create a focal point, mark an entry, attract a family of birds, or light the way for visitors. As a centerpiece, a stone sculpture can add to the illusion of timelessness a successful garden conveys. For pure whimsy, however, nothing surpasses a charming animal or figure placed as if by accident, tucked behind a tree or around the bend where a passerby least expects to find it.

Even functional additions to the garden can be chosen with an eye for their decorative attributes. Well-weathered lighting ~ a wooden lamppost aged to a silvery gray and topped by a copper-turned-verdigris fixture, for instance ~ fits in particularly well with a country setting. Lanterns and carriage lamps reproduced from Early American designs are also widely available and will add a nostalgic touch.

Birdhouses, bird feeders, and birdbaths also can be pleasing to look at as well as useful. Birdhouses encourage certain birds to prolong their visits; in return for free shelter, these welcome dwellers dine on unwanted insects, fill the air with song, and supply an endless source of fascination to birdwatchers.

Among the birds that can be lured into setting up

MEN OF STRAW

Quintessential "country," a gangly scarecrow asserting his authority over a field of corn has been a familiar sight for generations. Early settlers in America brought the tradition of a scarecrow, or "bird scarer," from their homelands, where straw men dressed in old clothes, usually with a turnip or gourd for a head, were a holdover from medieval times.

As seed-eating birds were a constant threat to new crops, making a scarecrow to frighten away feathered marauders became a springtime ritual. Friendly competitions often developed between neighbors, whose scarecrow characters were shaped by native traditions. The Germanic farmers who settled Pennsylvania, for example, fashioned the traditional *Bootzamon*, or bogey man, whose body was a wooden cross, crowned with a mop-top head and a hat of wool or straw.

A convocation of newly minted weathervanes takes place in a country meadow (left). Time-honored designs include a fire engine, banner, cow, arrow, deer, and stylized rooster. When properly mounted like the squirrel (above left), weathervanes are more than ornamental; they indicate a sudden change in wind direction that can mean a temperature drop or impending rain. A traditional copper lantern (above right) has weathered to a beautiful blue-green patina. The design of a backyard birdbath (opposite) provides a welcome spot for birds to splash. For centuries, bee skeps like the one in the foreground have found a place in country gardens. These domes of twisted straw are still used for hives today.

housekeeping are purple martins, robins, warblers, wrens, swallows, and bluebirds. Each has special housing needs. Martins, for instance, nest in groups and thus require a dwelling comprising at least four large rooms. Balconies and other projections where these very social birds can roost will also encourage martins to make their home in a country garden.

No matter what species of bird they are designed to attract, all birdhouses should be carefully positioned in a protected area out of the wind, and in partial shade so that the interior does not become too hot. Holes are needed for ventilation and drainage, and a small overhang above the entrance will help keep out the rain and discourage predators. (The interior should never be painted, as the fumes can harm birds.)

Feathered friends also enjoy a cooling splash in a birdbath placed in a shady spot. Not only will such garden ornaments bring pleasure to birds, but they also can be sculptures in themselves, punctuating the end of a path or the center of a flower bed. The location of birdhouses and baths may require some experimentation and flexibility before the new inhabitants are satisfied. Many birdwatchers will position a birdbath where it can be seen from a window in the house ~ always keeping a pair of binoculars close at hand.

When designed with character, birdhouses add personality and style to any country garden. Clockwise from opposite top left: a miniature church; a little white cottage with a green shake roof; a rustic Adirondack cabin modeled after a lodge in upstate New York; and a thatched cottage with a homey look. Multi-family housing for birds (above) includes boxes of many designs intended for a variety of species.

PLANTING FOR BIRDS AND BUTTERFLIES

A delight to the eye, birds and butterflies are also practical assets in a garden. Birds are especially useful in devouring annoying insects such as mosquitoes - along with their eggs and larvae - while butterflies help increase the flower population through their pollinating powers.

Since both these types of winged creatures are attracted to certain flowers, fruits, vegetables, and shrubs, it is possible to lure them into your yard by planting with their tastes in mind. Butterflies, for example, are drawn to strongly perfumed mauve and yellow flowers, and while still in their caterpillar stage will feast on nasturtiums and members of the cabbage family. Birds come in search of colorful berries and other fruits. Hummingbirds, of course, seek the sweet nectar of flowers, especially the blossoms of the trumpet vine (the red-orange color is their favorite).

For suggested plants for attracting birds and butterflies, see the Plant Lists at back of the book.

chapter six

PLANT LIST AND BIBLIOGRAPHY

If the preceding pages have inspired you, the pages that follow may help to make that inspiration a reality. In the plant list, a wide variety of plants for special situations are recommended. Shrubs that add color to the winter garden, for example, and fast-growing, fragrant vines are noted, together with reliable choices for virtually every color of climbing rose, plants that attract songbirds, and those that beckon butterflies. And, in a lively bibliography, we've collected our favorite gardening books—some years old and still wonderfully helpful.

Plant Lists

The following plant lists offer useful suggestions, and further research will help you determine if a particular plant is suited to your own garden. Appropriate hybrids or varieties are noted, otherwise, several kinds within a species may be effective. The horticultural dictionary, *Hortus Third*, is an excellent source for details on all types of plants cultivated in North America. Also, consult hardiness zone maps, available from your local Agricultural Extension Service, which provide the average minimum temperature in a specific region.

The following codes signify plant type:
(A) Annual; (BI) Biennial; (P) Perennial; (S) Shrub; (T) Tree

Plants for Drying

Flowers and stems are the most suitable parts unless seed pods or foliage are noted.

ANNUALS

Ageratum *(A. houstonianum)*; **Apple-of-Peru** *(Nicandra physalodes)*, pods; **Bachelor's Button** *(Centaurea cyanus)*; **Bishop's Flower** *(Ammi majus)*; **Cockscomb** *(Celosia argentea* var. *cristata)*; **Everlasting** *(Helipterum roseum)*; **Feathered Celosia** *(C. argentea plumosa)*; **Flowering Dill** *(Anethum graveolens)*; **Globe Amaranth** *(Gomphrena globosa)*; **Helipterum** *(H. humboldtianum)*; **Honesty** *(Lunaria annua)*, pods; **Hop Vine** *(Humulus)*, flowers, foliage; **Immortelle** *(Xeranthemum annuum)*; **Jerusalem Oak** *(Chenopodium botrys)*, flowers, foliage; **Love-in-a-mist** *(Nigella damascena)*, flowers, pods; **Love-lies-bleeding** *(Amaranthus caudatus)*; **Mealy-cup Sage** *(Salvia farinacea)* (P grown as half-hardy A); **Ornamental Corn** *(Zea mays)*; **Pansy** *(Viola × wittrockiana)*, (P grown as hardy A); **Pot Marigold** *(Calendula officinalis)*; **Rocket Larkspur** *(Consolida ambigua)*; **Rose-scented Geranium** *(Pelargonium graveolens)* (tender P grown as tender A), scented foliage; **Scabiosa** *(S. stellata)*, pods; **Statice** *(Limonium sinuatum)* (BI grown as tender A); **Strawflower** *(Helichrysum bracteatum)*; **Swan River Everlasting** or **Rhodanthe** *(Helipterum manglesii)*; **Wheat Celosia** *(C. argentea forma spicata)*; **Winged Everlasting** *(Ammobium alatum)*.

PERENNIALS

Artemisia *(Artemisia)*, foliage; **Astilbe** *(Astilbe × arendsii)*; **Baby's-breath** *(Gypsophila paniculata)*; **Bee Balm** *(Monarda didyma)*, flowers, pods; **Blanket Flower** *(Gaillardia)*, pods; **Butterfly Weed** *(Asclepias tuberosa)*; **Cardoon** *(Cynara cardunculus)*; **Carline Thistle** *(Carlina acaulis)*; **Chinese Lantern** *(Physalis alkekengi)*, pods; **Chive** *(Allium schoenoprasum)*; **Columbine** *(Aquilegia)*; **Cupid's Dart** *(Catananche caerula)*, pods; **Delphinium** *(Delphinium × cultorum)*; **Feverfew** *(Chrysanthemum parthenium)*; **Fountain Grass** *(Pennisetum alopecuroides* 'Burgundy Giant'*)*; **Gayfeather** *(Liatris)*; **German** or **Tatarian Statice** *(Goniolimon tataricum)*; **Globe Artichoke** *(Cynara scolymus)*, flowers, buds; **Globe Thistle** *(Echinops ritro)*; **Heather** *(Calluna)*; **Lady's Mantle** *(Alchemilla)*; **Lamb's Ear** *(Stachys byzantina)*, foliage; **Lavender** *(Lavandula angustifolia)*; **Loosestrife** *(Lythrum)*; **Oriental Poppy** *(Papaver orientale)*, pod; **Pearly Everlasting** *(Anaphalis margaritacea)*; **Peony** *(Paeonia)*; **Periwinkle** *(Vinca)*, foliage; **Plume Thistle** *(Cirsium japonicum)*; **Purple Coneflower** *(Echinacea purpurea)*; **Russian Sage** *(Perovskia atriplicifolia)*, flowers, foliage; **Santolina** *(S. chamaecyparissus)*, flowers, foliage; **Sea Holly** *(Eryngium)*; **Sea Lavender** *(Limonium)*; **Spearmint** *(Mentha spicata)*, flowers, foliage; **Thrift** *(Armeria)*; **Thyme** *(Thymus)*, flowers, foliage; **Yarrow** *(Achillea)*.

TREES & SHRUBS

Eucalyptus *(E. cinerea)*, foliage; **Hydrangea** *(Hydrangea)*; **Pussy Willow** *(Salix discolor)*, flowers, pods; **Rose** *(Rosa)*; flowers, hips; **Staghorn Sumac** *(Rhus typhina)*, berries; **Sugar Maple** *(Acer saccharum)*, fall foliage.

Shrubs for Color

FALL INTEREST

American Cranberrybush *(Viburnum trilobum)*, red berries and foliage; **Arrowwood Viburnum** *(V. dentatum)*, red foliage, blue-black berries; **Cranberry Cotoneaster** *(C. apiculatus)*, scarlet berries; **Doublefile Viburnum** *(V. plicatum* var. *tomentosum)*, red-purple foliage; **Ghent Hybrid Azalea** *(Rhododendron ×*

gandavense 'Corneille'), red-purple foliage; **Golden Currant** *(Ribes aureum)*, yellow-orange foliage; **Large Fothergilla** *(F. major)*, red foliage; **Nannyberry** *(Viburnum lentago)*, blue-black berries; **Purple Beautyberry** *(Callicarpa dichotoma)*, dark-red berries; **Sapphire Berry** *(Symplocos paniculata)*, blue berries; **Snowberry** *(Symphoricarpos albus)*, white berries; **Staghorn Sumac** *(Rhus typhina)*, red foliage; **Winterberry** *(Ilex verticillata)*, red berries.

WINTER INTEREST

Amur Privet *(Ligustrum amurense)*, black berries; **Chinese Witch Hazel** *(Hamamelis mollis)*, yellow flowers; **Goat Willow** *(Salix caprea)*, yellow flowers; **Japanese Barberry** *(Berberis thunbergii)*, red berries; **Japanese Skimmia** *(S. japonica)*, red berries; **Siberian Dogwood** *(Cornus alba* 'Sibirica'), red bark; **Winged Euonymus** *(E. alata)*, cork-like bark; **Yellow-twig Dogwood** *(Cornus sericea* 'Flaviramea'), yellow bark.

SPRING INTEREST

Azalea *(Rhododendron)*, white, pink, coral, orange, red, yellow, or lavender flowers; **Beautybush** *(Kolkwitzia amabilis)*, pink flowers; **Bridalwreath Spirea** *(Spiraea prunifolia)*, white flowers; **Cornelian Cherry** *(Cornus mas)*, yellow flowers; **Deutzia** *(Deutzia)*, white or pale-pink flowers; **February Daphne** *(D. mezereum)*, lilac or rose-purple flowers; **Flowering Currant** *(Ribes sanguineum)*, red flowers; **Flowering Quince** *(Chaenomeles speciosa)*, white, pink, or scarlet flowers; **Forsythia** *(Forsythia)*, yellow flowers; **Korean-spice Viburnum** *(V. carlesii)*, pale-pink flowers; **Large Fothergilla** *(F. major)*, white flowers; **Lilac** *(Syringa)*, purple, white, pink, lavender flowers; **Vanhoutte Spirea** *(Spiraea × vanhouttei)*, white flowers.

SUMMER INTEREST

American Elder *(Sambucus canadensis)*, white flowers; **Bluebeard** *(Caryopteris × clandonensis)*, blue flowers; **Bumald Spirea** *(Spiraea × bumalda* 'Anthony Waterer'), pink flowers; **Bush Cinquefoil** *(Potentilla fruticosa)*, yellow flowers; **Butterfly Bush** *(Buddleia davidii)*, lilac, pink, or reddish-purple flowers; **Chaste Tree** *(Vitex agnus-castus)*, lilac-blue or white flowers; **Crape Myrtle** *(Lagerstroemia indica)*, white, pink, red, or lavender flowers; **Hydrangea** *(Hydrangea)*, white, pink, blue, mauve flowers; **Rose of Sharon** *(Hibiscus syriacus)*, pink, red, purple, or white flowers; **Summersweet** *(Clethra alnifolia)*, white or pale-pink flowers; **Tatarian Honeysuckle** *(Lonicera tatarica)*, pink or red flowers, red or yellow berries; **Weigela** *(Weigela)*, white, pink, or red flowers.

YELLOW FOLIAGE

Golden Mock Orange (*Philadelphus coronarius* 'Aureus'); **Moonlight Holly** *(Ilex aquifolium* 'Flavescens'); **Spring Heath** *(Erica carnea* 'Aurea'); **Vicary Golden Privet** *(Ligustrum × vicaryi)*.

SILVER OR GRAY-BLUE FOLIAGE

Butterfly Bush *(Buddleia alternifolia* 'Argentea'); **Rue** *(Ruta graveolens)*; **Santolina** *(S. chamaecyparissus)*; **Senecio** *(S. greyi)*.

RED OR PURPLE FOLIAGE

Barberry *(Berberis thunbergii* 'Atropurpurea'); **Euonymus** *(E. europaea* 'Atropurpurea'); **Purple Weigela** *(W. florida* 'Foliis Purpuriis'); **Red-leaf Rose** *(Rosa rubrifolia)*.

VARIEGATED FOLIAGE

Barberry *(Berberis thunbergii* 'Rose Glow'); **Dogwood** *(Cornus alba* 'Spaethii'); **Eleagnus** *(Elaeagnus pungens* 'Variegata').

Ground Covers

PERENNIALS

Aubrieta *(A. deltoidea)*, sun; **Bergenia** *(B. cordifolia)*, light shade; **Black Mondo Grass** *(Ophiopogon planisapus* 'Arabicus'), partial shade; **Bugleweed** *(Ajuga reptans)*, light shade/sun; **Camomile** *(Chamaemelum nobile)*, sun; **Catmint** *(Nepeta mussinii)*, sun; **Coral Bell** *(Heuchera sanguinea)*, sun/light shade; **Cranesbill** *(Geranium)*, sun/light shade; **Daylily** *(Hemerocallis)*, sun/light shade; **Dead Nettle** *(Lamium maculatum)*, shade; **Epimedium** *(Epimedium)*, shade; **Forget-me-not** *(Brunnera macrophylla)*, shade; **Hay-scented Fern** *(Dennstaedtia punctilobula)*, sun/shade; **Hosta** *(Hosta)*, shade/light shade; **Japanese Painted Fern** *(Athyrium goeringianum* 'Pictum'), partial shade; **Lady Fern** *(Athyrium filix-femina)*, light shade; **Lamb's Ear** *(Stachys byzantina)*, sun; **Leadwort** *(Ceratostigma plumbaginoides)*, sun; **Lily-of-the-valley** *(Convallaria majalis)*, light shade; **Lilyturf** *(Liriope muscari)*, sun/light shade; **Lungwort** *(Pulmonaria saccharata)*, shade; **Moneywort** *(Lysimachia nummularia)*, sun/light shade; **Moss Phlox** *(P. subulata)*, sun/partial shade; **Pachysandra** *(P. terminalis)*, shade; **Periwinkle** *(Vinca)*, sun/shade; **Rock Cress** *(Arabis caucasica)*, sun; **Rock Rose** (*Helianthemum nummularium)*, sun; **Saxifrage** *(Saxifraga)*, shade; **Sea Pink** *(Armeria maritima)*, sun; **Serbian Bellflower** *(Campanula poscharskyana)*, sun/light shade; **Sheep's Fescue** *(Festuca ovina* 'Glauca Minima'), sun/light shade; **Snow-in-summer** *(Cerastium tomentosum)*, sun; **Stonecrop** *(Sedum)*, sun; **Sweet Woodruff** *(Galium odoratum)*, light shade; **Veronica** *(V. pectinata)*, sun; **Violet** *(Viola odorata, V. blanda)*, shade/light shade; **Wild Ginger** *(Asarum europaeum)*, shade; **Woolly Thyme** *(Thymus pseudolanuginosus)*, sun; **Yellow Archangel** *(Lamiastrum galeobdolon)*, shade.

SHRUBS

Bearberry *(Arctostaphylos uva-ursi)*, sun/light shade; **Broom** *(Cytisus purpureus)*, sun; **Bush**

Cinquefoil *(Potentilla fruticosa)*, sun; **Cotoneaster** *(C. horizontalis, C. salicifolius)*, sun/light shade; **Creeping Dogwood** *(Cornus canadensis)*, light shade; **Creeping Mahonia** *(M. repens)*, shade/sun; **David Viburnum** *(V. davidii)*, sun/light shade; **Euonymous** *(E. fortunei)*, sun/shade; **Heath** or **Heather** *(Calluna)*, sun; **Honeysuckle** *(Lonicera prostrata)*, sun/shade; **Juniper** *(Juniperus horizontalis)*, sun/light shade; **Memorial Rose** *(Rosa wichuraiana)*, sun; **St. John's Wort** *(Hypericum calycinum)*, sun/shade; **Santolina** *(S. chamaecyparissus)*, sun; **Spreading English Yew** *(Taxus baccata* 'Repandens'*)*, sun/shade; **Trailing Rosemary** *(Rosmarinus officinalis* 'Prostratus'*)*, sun; **Wintergreen** *(Gaultheria procumbens)*, light shade.

VINES

Clematis *(Clematis)*, sun/partial shade; **Climbing Hydrangea** *(H. anomala petiolaris)*, sun; **Crimson Vine** *(Vitis coignetiae)*, sun; **Henry Honeysuckle** *(Lonicera henryi)*, sun/shade; **Ivy** *(Hedera)*, shade/sun; **Perennial Pea** *(Lathyrus latifolius)*, sun; **Virginia Creeper** *(Parthenocissus quinquefolia)*, sun/shade.

Low-maintenance Annuals

*Plants that are tender perennials or perennials commonly grown as annuals.

Ageratum *(A. houstonianum)*; **Bachelor's Button** *(Centaurea cyanus)*; **Blanket Flower** *(Gaillardia amblyodon, G. puchella)*; **Blue Lace Flower** *(Trachymene coerulea)*; ***California Poppy** *(Eschscholzia californica)*; **Cleome** *(C. hasslerana)*; **Cockscomb** *(Celosia argentea* var. *cristata)*; ***Coleus** *(C. blumei)*; **Cosmos** *(C. bipinnatus)*; ***Cup-and-saucer Vine** *(Cobaea scandens)*; **Dianthus** *(D. barbatus, D. chinensis)*; ***Flowering Maple** *(Abutilon hybridum)*; ***Gazania** *(G. longiscapa)*; **Gypsophila** *(G. elegans)*; ***Heliotrope** *(Heliotropium arborescens)*; ***Hyacinth Bean Vine** *(Dolichos lablab)*; ***Impatiens** *(I. balsamina, I. wallerana)*; **Larkspur** *(Consolida)*; **Linaria** *(L. maroccana)*; **Marigold** *(Tagetes)*; **Mexican Sunflower** *(Tithonia rotundifolia)*; ***Mimulus** *(Mimulus × hybridus grandiflorus)*; **Moonflower** *(Ipomoea alba)*; **Morning Glory Vine** *(Ipomoea purpurea)*; **Nasturtium** *(Tropaeolum majus)*; **Nicotiana** *(N. alata)*; **Pansy** *(Viola × wittrockiana)*; **Petunia** *(Petunia × hybrida)*; **Phlox** *(P. drummondii)*; **Portulaca** *(P. grandiflora)*; ***Salvia** *(S. horminum)*; **Scabiosa** *(S. atropurpurea)*; ***Snapdragon** *(Antirrhinum majus)*; **Statice** *(Limonium sinuata)*; **Stock** *(Matthiola)*; **Sunflower** *(Helianthus annuus)*; ***Sweet Alyssum** *(Lobularia maritima)*; **Tahoka Daisy** *(Aster tanacetifolius)*; **Torenia** *(T. fournieri)*; **Verbena** *(V. hortensis)*; ***Wax Begonia** *(Begonia × semperflorens-cultorum)*; **Zinnia** *(Z. elegans)*.

Vines

PERENNIAL VINES NOTABLE FOR FLOWERS

Blue Passion Flower *(Passiflora caerulea)*; **Cape Plumbago** *(P. auriculata)*; **Carolina Jasmine** *(Gelsemium sempervirens)*; **Cinnamon Vine** *(Dioscorea batatas)*; **Clematis** *(Clematis)*; **Climbing Hydrangea** *(H. anomala petiolaris)*; **Common White Jasmine** *(Jasminum officinale)*; **Coral Vine** *(Antigonon leptopus)*; **Cross Vine** *(Bignonia capreolata)*; **Golden Trumpet Allamanda** *(A. carthartica)*; **Honeysuckle** *(Lonicera)*; **Perennial Pea** *(Lathyrus latifolius)*; **Silver Lace Vine** *(Polygonum aubertii)*; **Wisteria** *(Wisteria)*.

PERENNIAL LEAFY OR BERRIED VINES

American Bittersweet *(Celastrus scandens)*; **Boston Ivy** *(Parthenocissus tricuspidata)*; **Bower Actinidia** *(A. arguta)*; **Common Hop** *(Humulus lupulus)*; **Five-leaf Akebia** *(A. quinata)*; **Dutchman's Pipe** *(Aristolochia durior)*; **Euonymus** *(E. fortunei)*; **Grape** *(Vitis)*; **Ivy** *(Hedera)*; **Porcelain Vine** *(Ampelopsis brevipedunculata)*; **Virginia Creeper** *(Parthenocissus quinquefolia)*.

ANNUAL VINES

Balloon Vine *(Cardiospermum halicacabum)*; **Black-eyed Susan Vine** *(Thunbergia alata)*; **Cup-and-saucer Vine** *(Cobaea scandens)*; **Hyacinth Bean** *(Dolichos lablab)*; **Japanese Hop** *(Humulus scandens)*; **Mock Cucumber** *(Echinocystus lobata)*; **Moonflower** *(Ipomoea alba)*; **Morning Glory** *(Ipomoea tricolor, I. purpurea)*; **Nasturtium** *(Tropaeolum majus)*; **Scarlet Runner Bean** *(Phaseolus coccineus)*; **Sweet Pea** *(Lathyrus odoratus)*.

Fragrant Border Plants

BULBS, CORMS & RHIZOMES

Abyssinian Gladiolus or Peacock Orchid *(Acideranth a bicolor)*; **Bluebell** *(Hyacinthoides non-scripta)*; **Grape Hyacinth** *(Muscari armeniacum, M. moschatum)*; **Hardy Cyclamen** *(C. hederifolium)*; **Hyacinth** *(Hyacinthus orientalis)*; **Iris** *(Iris × germanica, I. pallida)*; **Narcissus** *(N. jonquilla, N. poeticus recurvus, N. tazetta)*; **Snowdrop** *(Galanthus* 'S. Arnott'*)*; **Tulip** *(Tulipa sylvestris, T. tarda)* hybrids: 'De Wet', 'Bellona'.

ANNUALS & BIENNIALS

Black Cosmos *(C. atrosanguineus)*; **Evening Primrose** *(Oenothera caespitosa)*; **Heliotrope** *(Heliotropium arborescens)*; **Mignonette** *(Reseda odorata)*; **Nasturtium** *(Tropaeolum majus)*; **Nicotiana** *(N. alata)*; **Phlox** *(P. drummondii)*; **Pot Marigold** *(Calendula officinalis)*; **Purple Basil** *(Ocimum basilicum* 'Dark Opal'*)*; **Rocket Candytuft** *(Iberis amara)*; **Snapdragon** *(Antirrhinum majus)*; **Stock** *(Matthiola bicornis, M. incana)*; **Sweet Alyssum** *(Lobularia maritima)*; **Verbena** *(Verbena × hybrida)*; **Wallflower** *(Cheiranthus cheiri)*.

PERENNIALS

Bay Laurel *(Laurus nobilis)* (S); **Boxwood** *(Buxus sempervirens)* (S); **Calamint** *(Calamintha)*; **Camomile** *(Chamaemelum nobile)*; **Catmint** *(Nepeta × faassenii)*; **Cheddar Pink** *(Dianthus gratianopolitanus)*; **Corsican Mint** *(Mentha requienii)*; **Cowslip** *(Primula veris)*; **Cranesbill** *(Geranium endressii* 'Wargrave Pink*)*; **Hosta** *(H. plantaginea)*; **Hyssop** *(Hyssopus officinalis)*, subshrub; **Lavender** *(Lavandula angustifolia)*, subshrub; **Lemon Daylily** *(Hemerocallis flava)*; **Lemon Thyme** *(Thymus × citriodorus)*; **Lily-of-the-valley** *(Convallaria majalis)*; **Rose** *(Rosa* 'Rise `N Shine'*)* (S); **Rosemary** *(Rosmarinus officinalis)*, subshrub; **Sweet Violet** *(Viola odorata)*; **Sweet William** *(Dianthus barbatus)*; **Sweet Woodruff** *(Galium odoratum)*.

CLIMBING ROSES

White – 'Cherokee', 'City of York', 'Paul's Lemon Pillar', 'Silver Moon'; **Yellow** – 'Golden Showers', 'High Noon', 'Lawrence Johnston'; **Cream edged with Pink** – 'Handel'; **Yellow turning Red** – 'Joseph's Coat'; **Apricot** – 'Alchymist'; **Pale Pink** – 'Climbing Cecile Brunner', 'New Dawn'; **Pale Pink turning Creamy White** – 'Madame Alfred Carrière'; **Medium Pink** – 'Blossomtime', 'Dr. J.H. Nicholas', 'Jeanne Lajoie' (miniature), 'May Queen'; **Deep Pink** – 'American Pillar', 'Coral Dawn', 'Viking Queen'; **Coral Salmon** – 'America'; **Red and White** – 'Dortmund'; **Red** – 'Blaze'; **Crimson to Maroon** – 'Don Juan', 'Dr. Huey'.

Container Plants

ANNUALS

Ageratum *(A. houstonianum)*; **Blue Lace Flower** *(Trachymene coerulea)*; **Blue Marguerite** *(Felicia amelloides)*; **Bush Violet** *(Browallia)*; **Cosmos** *(C. bipinnatus)*; **Cupflower** *(Nierembergia scoparia)*; **Geranium** *(Pelar-gonium)*; **Helichrysum** *(H. petiolatum)*; **Heliotrope** *(Heliotropium arborescens)*; **Impatiens** *(I. wallerana)*; **Lobelia** *(Lobelia)*; **Marigold** *(Tagetes)*; **Nasturtium** *(Tropaeolum majus)*; **Nemesia** *(Nemesia)*; **Nicotiana** *(N. alata)*; **Ornamental Kale** *(Brassica oleracea)*; **Pansy** *(Viola × wittrockiana)*; **Petunia** *(Petunia × hybrida)*; **Phlox** *(P. drummondi)*; **Portulaca** *(P. grandiflora)*; **Pot Marigold** *(Calendula officinalis)*; **Snapdragon** *(Antirrhinum majus)*; **Sunflower** *(Helianthus annuus)*; **Sweet Alyssum** *(Lobularia maritima)*; **Sweet William** *(Dianthus barbatus)*; **Verbena** *(Verbena × hybrida)*; **Zinnia** *(Z. elegans)*.

PERENNIALS & HERBS

Catmint *(Nepeta mussinii)*; **Chive** *(Allium schoenoprasum)*; **Hosta** *(Hosta)*; **Houseleek** *(Sempervivum)*; **Hyssop** *(Hyssopus officinalis)*; **Lamb's Ear** *(Stachys byzantina)*; **Lavender** *(Lavandula)*; **Leadwort** *(Ceratostigma plumbaginoides)*; **Loosestrife** *(Lythrum)*; **Mint** *(Mentha)*; **Rosemary** *(Rosmarinus officinalis)*; **Stonecrop** *(Sedum)*; **Strawberry** *(Fragaria)*; **Veronica** *(Veronica)*; **Wax Begonia** *(Begonia × semperflorens-cultorum)*.

VINES

Bougainvillea *(Bougainvillea)* (P); **Clematis** *(Clematis)* (P); **Golden Trumpet Allamanda** *(A. cathartica)* (P); **Honeysuckle** *(Lonicera)* (P); **Hop** *(Humulus)* (P); **Ivy** *(Hedera)* (P); **Jasmine** *(Jasminum)* (P); **Mock Cucumber** *(Echinocystus lobata)* (A); **Morning Glory** *(Ipomoea purpurea)* (A); **Passion Flower** *(Passiflora)* (P); **Scarlet Runner Bean** *(Phaseolus coccineus)* (A).

SHRUBS & TREES

Abutilon or **Flowering Maple** *(Abutilon)*; **Apple and Crabapple** *(Malus)*; **Azalea** *(Rhododendron)*; **Bay** *(Laurus nobilis)*; **Boxwood** *(Buxus)*; **Camellia** *(C. japonica)*; **Cotoneaster** *(Cotoneaster)*; **Cypress** *(Cupressus)*; **Fuchsia** *(Fuchsia)*; **Gardenia** *(G. jasminoides)*; **Holly** *(Ilex)*; **Hydrangea** *(Hydrangea)*; **Japanese Maple** *(Acer palmatum)*; **Juniper** *(Juniperus)*; **Lantana** *(Lantana)*; **Lemon** *(Citrus limon)*; **Lilac** *(Syringa)*; **Oleander** *(Nerium oleander)*; **Orange** *(Citrus sinensis)*; **Rose** *(Rosa)*; **Tree Mallow** *(Malva)*; **Viburnum** *(Viburnum)*; **Yew** *(Taxus)*.

BULBS, CORMS, RHIZOMES & TUBERS

Agapanthus *(Agapanthus)*; **Allium** *(Allium)*; **Crocus** *(Crocus)*; **Cyclamen** *(Cyclamen)*; **Dahlia** *(Dahlia)*; **Gladiolus** *(Gladiolus)*; **Grape Hyacinth** *(Muscari)*; **Iris** *(Iris)*; **Lily** *(Lilium)*; **Narcissus** *(Narcissus)*; **Squill** *(Scilla)*; **Tuberous Begonia** *(Begonia × tuberhybrida)*; **Tulip** *(Tulipa)*.

WATER PLANTS

Hardy or **Tropical Water Lily** *(Nymphaea)*; **Hardy Water Canna** *(Thalia dealbata)*; **Lotus** *(Nelumbo)*; **Miniature Cattail** *(Typha minima)*.

Plants for Attracting Birds

HUMMINGBIRD PLANTS

Hummingbirds are particularly attracted to the color red.

Beautybush *(Kolkwitzia amabilis)* (S); **Bee Balm** *(Monarda didyma* 'Cambridge Scarlet'*)* (P); **Cardinal Flower** or **Lobelia** *(L. cardinalis)* (P); **Columbine** *(Aquilegia)* (P); **Coralberry** *(Symphoricarpos orbiculatus)* (S); **Fireweed** *(Epilobium angustifolium)* (P); **Four O'Clock** *(Mirabilis jalapa)* (A); **Hollyhock** *(Alcea)* (BI) or (P); **Mexican Sunflower** *(Tithonia rotundifolia)* (A); **Mint** *(Mentha)* (P); **Nicotiana** *(N. alata)* (A); **Petunia** *(Petunia × hybrida)* (A); **Scarlet Bugler Penstemon** *(P. barbatus)* (P); **Scarlet Sage** *(Salvia splendens)* (A); **Scarlet Trumpet Honeysuckle** *(Lonicera sempervirens)* (P), vine; **Trumpet Creeper** *(Campsis radicans)* (P), vine; **Weigela** (Weigela) (S).

Songbird Flowers

The following flowers produce seeds that attract songbirds.

Aster *(Aster)* (P); **Bachelor's Button** *(Centaurea cyanus)* (A); **Bellflower** *(Campanula)* (P); **Black-eyed Susan** *(Rudbeckia fulgida)* (P); **Campion** *(Silene schafta)* (P); **Chrysanthemum** *(Chrysanthemum)* (P); **Coreopsis** *(Coreopsis)* (P); **Cosmos** *(Cosmos)* (A); **Flax** *(Linum)* (P); **Love-lies-bleeding** *(Amaranthus caudatus)* (A); **Portulaca** *(P. grandifiora)* (A); **Phlox,** *(P. drummondii)* (A); **Poppy** *(Papaver)* (A) (BI) (P); **Pot Marigold** *(Calendula officinalis)* (A); **Sunflower** *(Helianthus annuus)* (A); **Verbena** *(Verbena × hybrida)* (P); **Zinnia** *(Z. elegans)* (A).

BIRD PLANTS

These attract birds by providing shelter or food.

Bayberry *(Myrica)* (S); **Blueberry** *(Vaccinium)* (S); **Cotoneaster** *(Cotoneaster)* (S); **Crabapple** *(Malus)* (T); **Currant** *(Ribes)* (S); **Dogwood** *(Cornus)* (T); **Elderberry** *(Sambucus)* (S); **Firethorn** *(Pyracantha)* (S); **Grape** *(Vitis)* (P), vine; **Hackberry** *(Celtis occidentalis)* (T); **Hawthorn** *(Crataegus)* (T); **Holly** *(Ilex)* (S) (T); **Juniper** *(Juniperus)* (S) (T); **Mountain Ash** *(Sorbus americana)* (T); **Rose** *(Rosa)* (S); **Serviceberry** *(Amelanchier)* (T); **Snowberry** *(Symphoricarpos albus)* (S); **Sour Gum** *(Nyssa)* (T); **Sumac** *(Rhus)* (S); **Tatarian Honeysuckle** *(Lonicera tatarica)* (S); **Viburnum** *(Viburnum)* (S); **Virginian Bird Cherry** *(Prunus virginiana)* (T); **Virginia Creeper** *(Parthenocissus quinquefolia)* (P), vine.

Plants for Attracting Butterflies

FLOWERS

Aubrieta *(Aubrieta)* (P); **Aster** *(Aster)* (P); **Astilbe** *(Astilbe)* (P); **Basket-of-gold** *(Aurinia saxatilis)* (P); **Bee Balm** *(Monarda didyma)* (P); **Bellflower** *(Campanula)* (P); **Blanket Flower** *(Gaillardia)* (P); **Butterfly Weed** *(Asclepias tuberosa)* (P); **Coreopsis** *(C. verticillata)* (P); **Cosmos** *(C. hybrida)* (A); **Dame's Rocket** *(Hesperis matronalis)* (P); **Dianthus** *(D. plumarius)* (P); **Evergreen Candytuft** *(Iberis sempervirens)* (P); **Gayfeather** *(Liatris spicata)* (P); **Heliotrope** *(Heliotropium arborescens)* (A); **Jacob's Ladder** *(Polemonium caeruleum)* (P); **Japanese Anemone** *(Anemone × hybrida)* (P); **Johnny-jump-up** *(Viola tricolor)* (A); **Lantana** *(Lantana)* (A); **Lupine** *(Lupinus)* (A); **Marigold** *(Tagetes)* (A); **Meadow Rue** *(Thalictrum)* (P); **Mexican Sunflower** *(Tithonia rotundifolia)* (A); **Nasturtium** *(Tropaeolum majus)* (A); **Petunia** *(Petunia)* (A); **Phlox** *(Phlox)* (P); **Purple Coneflower** *(Echinacea purpurea)* (P); **Red Valerian** *(Centranthus ruber)* (P); **Sage** *(Salvia)* (P); **Scabiosa** *(S. caucasica)* (P); **Sea Holly** *(Eryngium maritimum)* (P); **Shasta Daisy** *(Chrysanthemum × superbum)* (P); **Stonecrop** *(Sedum)* (P); **Sunflower** *(Helianthus annuus)* (A); **Sweet Alyssum** *(Lobularia maritima)* (A); **Verbena** *(Verbena × hybrida)* (A); **Yarrow** *(Achillea)* (P); **Zinnia** *(Zinnia)* (A).

VINES

Common Hop *(Humulus lupulus)* (P); **Dutchman's Pipe** *(Aristolochia durior)* (P); **Honeysuckle** *(Lonicera)* (P); **Passion Flower** *(Passiflora)* (P); **Sweet Pea** *(Lathyrus odoratus)* (A).

SHRUBS

Arrowwood Viburnum *(V. dentatum)*; **Butterfly Bush** *(Buddleia davidii)*; **Bluebeard** *(Caryopteris × clandonensis)*; **Chaste Tree** *(Vitex vagnus-castus)*; **Germander** *(Teucrium chamaedrys)*; **Lavender** *(Lavandula)*; **Lilac** *(Syringa)*; **Mock Orange** *(Philadelphus)*; **Privet** *(Ligustrum)*; **Rockrose** *(Cistus)*; **Rose of Sharon** *(Hibiscus syriacus)*; **Sweet Pepperbush** *(Clethra)*.

Bibliography

These are the books that inspire and guide us. Some of the classics may be out of print, but should be available at your local library or garden club.

Abraham, George and Katy Abraham et al. *Low-Maintenance Gardening.* Brooklyn Botanic Garden, 1987.

Bailey, Liberty Hyde and Ethel Zoe Bailey. *Hortus Third: A Concise Dictionary of Plants Cultivated in the United States and Canada.* Macmillan Publishing Co., 1976.

Bartholomew, Alexander et al. *Conservatories, Greenhouses and Garden Rooms.* Holt, Rinehart and Winston, 1985.

Barton, Barbara J. *Gardening By Mail.* Houghton Mifflin, 1990.

Beales, Peter. *Roses: An Illustrated Encyclopedia and Grower's Handbook of Species Roses. Old Roses and Modern Roses, Shrub Roses and Climbers.* Henry Holt & Co., 1992

Boisset, Caroline. *Vertical Gardening.* Weidenfeld & Nicolson, 1988.

Brickell, Christopher, editor-in-chief. *The American Horticultural Society: Encyclopedia of Garden Plants.* Macmillan Publishing Co., 1989.

Brookes, John. *The Country Garden.* Crown Publishers, 1987.

_____. *The Book of Garden Design.* Macmillan Publishing Co., 1991.

Bryan, John E., *Hearst Garden Guides, Bulbs.* Hearst Books, 1992.

Bush-Brown, James and Louise Bush-Brown. *America's Garden Book.* Charles Scribner's Sons, 1980.

Carley, Rachel. *The Backyard Book.* Viking, 1988.

Clausen, Ruth Rogers and Nicolas H. Ekstrom. *Perennials for American Gardens.* Random House, 1989.

Coats, Alice M. *Garden Shrubs and Their Histories.* Simon & Schuster, 1992.

Colborn, Nigel. *The Container Garden.* Little, Brown , 1990.

Coughlin, Roberta M. *The Gardener's Companion: A Book of Lists and Lore.* Harper Collins Publishers, 1991.

Cravens, Richard H. et al. *Vines: The Time-Life Encyclopedia of Gardening.* Time-Life Books, 1979.

Creasy, Rosalind. *Cooking from the Garden.* Sierra Club Books, 1988.

Cressy, Judith and Rosemary Rennicke et al. *The Country Garden.* Time-Life Books, 1989.

Crockett, James Underwood et al. *The Time-Life Encyclopedia of Gardening: Annuals; Evergreens; Flowering Shrubs; Lawns and Groundcovers; Landscape Gardening; Perennials.* Time-Life Books, 1971-72.

Damrosch, Barbara. *The Garden Primer.* Workman Publishing, 1988.

Davis, Brian. *The Gardener's Illustrated Encyclopedia of Trees and Shrubs: A Guide to More Than 2000 Varieties.* Rodale Press, 1987.

Dirr, Michael A. *Manual of Woody Landscape Plants: Their Identification, Ornamental Characteristics, Culture, Propagation and Uses.* Stipes Publishing Company, 1975.

Dobson, Beverly R. *Combined Rose List 1990.* Beverly R. Dobson, 1990 (available annually).

Druitt, Liz and G. Michael Shoup. *Landscaping with Antique Roses.* The Taunton Press, 1992.

Druse, Ken. *The Natural Shade Garden.* Clarkson N. Potter, 1992.

_____. *The Natural Garden.* Clarkson N. Potter, 1989.

Ely, Helena Rutherfurd. *A Woman's Hardy Garden.* Collier Books, 1990.

Fretwell, Barry. *Clematis.* Capability's Books, 1989.

Gardner, JoAnn. *The Heirloom Garden; Selecting and Growing Over 300 Old-Fashioned Ornamentals.* Garden Way Publishing, 1992

Garnock, Jamie. *Trellis: The Creative Way to Transform Your Garden.* Rizzoli, 1991.

Gault, S. Millar and Patrick M. Synge. *The Dictionary of Roses in Colour.* Michael Joseph, 1971.

Giblin, James and Dale Ferguson. *The Scarecrow Book.* Crown Publishers, 1980.

Hamilton, Geoff. *The Organic Garden Book.* Crown Publishers, 1987.

Harrod, Julie. *The Garden Wall.* The Atlantic Monthly Press, 1991.

Heriteau, Jacqueline with Dr. H. Marc Cathey. *The National Arboretum Book of Outstanding Garden Plants.* Simon & Schuster, 1990.

Hobhouse, Penelope. *Flower Gardens.* Little, Brown, 1991.

Huxley, Anthony, editor, et al. *The New Royal Horticultural Society Dictionary of Gardening.* The Stockton Press, 1992.

Hylton, William, editor. *Projects for Outdoor Living.* Rodale Press, 1990.

Johnson, Hugh. *The Principles of Gardening.* Simon & Schuster, 1979.

Keeling, Jim. *The Terracotta Gardener.* Trafalgar Square Publishing, 1990.

Knopf, Jim. *The Xeriscape Flower Gardener.* Johnson Books, 1991.

Kowalchik, Claire and William H. Hylton. *Rodale's Encyclopedia of Herbs.* Rodale Press, 1987.

Lacey, Stephen. *Scent in Your Garden.* Little, Brown, 1991

Lacy, Allen, editor. *The American Gardener: A Sampler.* Farrar, Straus, Giroux, 1988.

Lovejoy, Sharon. *Sunflower Houses: Garden Discoveries for Children of All Ages.* Interweave Press, 1991.

Perényi, Eleanor. *Green Thoughts: A Writer in the Garden.* Random House, 1981.

Phillips, Roger and Martyn Rix. *Bulbs.* Random House, 1981.

______. *Roses.* Random House, 1988.

Pollan, Michael. *Second Nature: A Gardener's Education.* The Atlantic Monthly Press, 1991.

Proctor, Dr. Noble. *Garden Birds.* Rodale Press, 1986.

Proctor, Rob. *Antique Flowers: Perennials.* Harper & Row, 1990.

Rix, Martyn. *Growing Bulbs.* Timber Press, 1983.

Rodale, J. I. et al. *How to Grow Vegetables and Fruits by the Organic Method.* Rodale Books, Inc., 1961.

Scanniello, Stephen and Tania Bayard. *Roses of America.* Henry Holt & Co., 1990.

Sedenko, Jerry. *The Butterfly Garden.* Villard Books, 1991.

Silber, Mark and Terry Silber. *The Complete Book of Everlastings.* Knopf, 1988.

Sinnes, A. Cort et al. *All About Fertilizers, Soils and Water.* Ortho Books, 1979.

______. *All About Perennials.* Ortho Books, 1981.

Smith, L. Ken et al. *Do-It-Yourself Garden Construction Know How.* Ortho Books, 1976.

Sunset Magazine et al. *Western Garden Book.* Lane Publishing Company, 1988.

Swindells, Philip. *Waterlilies.* Timber Press, 1983.

Tanner, Ogden. *Gardening America: Regional and Historical Influences in the Contemporary Garden.* Viking Studio Books, 1990.

Tanner, Ogden et al. *Garden Construction: The Time-Life Encyclopedia of Gardening.* Time-Life Books, 1978.

Taylor, Norman. Revised and edited by Gordon P. DeWolf, Jr. *Taylor's Guides: Annuals; Bulbs; Garden Design; Gardening Techniques; Ground Covers, Vines & Grasses; Perennials; Roses; Shrubs; Trees; Vegetables & Herbs; Water-Saving Gardening.* Houghton Mifflin, 1986-1991.

Tekulsky, Mathew. *The Butterfly Garden.* Harvard Common Press, 1985.

Thomas, R. William, *Hearst Garden Guides, Trees & Shrubs.* Hearst Books, 1992

Thaxter, Celia. *An Island Garden.* Bullbrier Press, 1985

Thomas, Graham Stuart. *Climbing Roses Old and New.* St. Martin's Press, 1965.

_____. *The Art of Gardening With Roses.* Henry Holt & Co., 1991.

Tolley, Emelie and Chris Mead. *Herbs: Gardens, Decorations, and Recipes.* Clarkson N. Potter, 1985.

Wilder, Louise Beebe. *Color In My Garden.* The Atlantic Monthly Press, 1990.

_____. *The Fragrant Garden.* Dover Publications, Inc., 1974.

Williams, Henry Lionel and Ottalie K. Williams. *A Guide to Old American Houses 1700-1900.* A. S. Barnes and Co., 1962.

Wilson, Helen Van Pelt and Léonie Bell. *The Fragrant Year.* M. Barrows & Company, Inc., 1967.

Woods, May and Arete Warren. *Glass Houses.* Rizzoli, 1988.

Wyman, Donald. *Wyman's Gardening Encyclopedia.* Macmillan Publishing Co., 1971.

Credits

Dirk Kramer and Terry Atkin, Architects
490 West End Avenue
New York, NY 10024
(Architectural design, pages 42–47)

Fisher & Chappell Paintworks
7637 Brockway Drive
Boulder, CO 80303
(Trompe l'oeil painting, pages 48–51)

Sonoma Flower Company
6683 Sonoma Highway
Santa Rosa, CA 95409
(Floral arrangements, pages 60–65)

Photography Credits

2	Keith Scott Morton
4–5	Keith Scott Morton
6	Keith Scott Morton (top left, bottom left) Jessie Walker (right)
7	Keith Scott Morton (top left, bottom left, right)
8	Jessie Walker
11–13	Keith Scott Morton
14–15	Cary Hazlegrove
16	Keith Scott Morton
17	Jerry Abromowitz
18	Charles Nesbitt
19	Keith Scott Morton
20	Jessie Walker
20–21	Keith Scott Morton
22–23	Rick Patrick
24	Jessie Walker
24–25	Arthur Griggs
26–28	Keith Scott Morton
29	Niña Williams
30–31	Jessie Walker
32	Keith Scott Morton
33	Doug Kennedy
34–35	Keith Scott Morton
36–41	Jessie Walker
42–47	Keith Scott Morton

48–54	Jessie Walker
55	Marc Horovitz (left)
	Jessie Walker (right)
56–57	Barbara Horovitz
58	Barbara Horovitz (top and bottom)
	Marc Horovitz (center)
59	Jessie Walker
60–63	Keith Scott Morton
64–65	A. Gridley Graves
66–67	Jessie Walker
68	Jeffrey Frank
69	Joshua Greene
70–73	Jeffrey Frank
74–76	Keith Scott Morton
77	Jeffrey Frank
78	Niña Williams
79	Jessie Walker
80–81	Keith Scott Morton
82	Jessie Walker (top left)
	Keith Scott Morton (top right)
	Doug Kennedy (bottom left and right)
83	Keith Scott Morton
84	Doug Kennedy
85	Rick Patrick (left and right)
86	Rick Patrick (left)
	Niña Williams (right)
87	Niña Williams
88	Rick Patrick (left)
	Jessie Walker (right)
89	Rick Patrick (top left, top right, bottom right)
	Keith Scott Morton (bottom left)
90	Jessie Walker
90–91	Charles Nesbit
92	Jessie Walker
93	Cary Hazlegrove
94	Keith Scott Morton (top left, top right)
	Niña Williams (bottom left, bottom right)
95	Jerry Abromowitz
96–97	Joseph V. Tomocik
98	Jessie Walker
99	Niña Williams (left)
	Jessie Walker (right)
100	Jessie Walker
101	Keith Scott Morton (top)
	André Gillardin (center)
	Rick Patrick (bottom)
102–104	Niña Williams
105–107	Keith Scott Morton
107	Niña Williams (center and right)
109	Jessie Walker
110	Keith Scott Morton
111	Jessie Walker
112–115	Keith Scott Morton
116	Jessie Walker (left)
	Keith Scott Morton (right)
117–120	Keith Scott Morton
121	Keith Scott Morton (top)
	Elyse Lewin (bottom)
122	Jessie Walker
122–123	Keith Scott Morton
124	Jessie Walker
125	Keith Scott Morton
126–127	Jessie Walker
128–129	Keith Scott Morton
130	Jessie Walker (top)
	George W. Gardner (bottom)
131–132	Keith Scott Morton
133	Jessie Walker
134–137	Keith Scott Morton
138	Keith Scott Morton (top)
	Jessie Walker (bottom)
139	Jessie Walker
140	Cary Hazlegrove (left)
	Jessie Walker (right)
141	Doug Kennedy
142	Paul Kopelow
143–144	Doug Kennedy
145–146	Jessie Walker
147	Keith Scott Morton (above)
	Paul Kopelow (bottom left)
	Jessie Walker (bottom right)
148–149	Jessie Walker
150–151	Keith Scott Morton
152–153	Jessie Walker
154	Keith Scott Morton
155	Jerry Abromowitz
156	Cary Hazlegrove
157	Paul Kopelow (top)
	Keith Scott Morton (center)
	Jessie Walker (bottom)
158	Jessie Walker
159	Doug Kennedy
160	Keith Scott Morton (left)
	Niña Williams
161	Keith Scott Morton
162	Jessie Walker
163	Cary Hazlegrove
164	Paul Kopelow
165	Keith Scott Morton (top)
	Jessie Walker (bottom)
166–167	Keith Scott Morton
168	Cary Hazlegrove
169	Jessie Walker
170–171	Paul Kopelow
172	Jessie Walker (top)
	Keith Scott Morton (bottom)
173	Jessie Walker
174	A. Gridley Graves
175	Paul Kopelow (top, bottom left)
	Niña Williams (bottom right)
176–177	Niña Williams
178–179	Jessie Walker
180	Rick Patrick
181	Jessie Walker (left)
	Doug Kennedy (top right)
	Keith Scott Morton (bottom right)
182	Doug Kennedy
183	Jessie Walker
184	Keith Scott Morton
185	Rick Patrick (left)
	Keith Scott Morton (right)
186	Rick Patrick (top left, top right, bottom left)
	Jessie Walker (bottom right)
187	Keith Scott Morton (top left, bottom)
	Rick Patrick (top right)
188	Pamela Landau (left)
	Jessie Walker (center)
	Keith Scott Morton (right)
189	Niña Williams
190	Doug Kennedy (top left)
	Keith Scott Morton (top right, bottom right)
	Niña Williams (bottom left)
191	Jessie Walker (left)
	Niña Williams (right)
192	Rick Patrick
194–201	Niña Williams

Acknowledgments

We would like to express our warm appreciation to all the avid country gardeners who shared their expertise during this project. We extend special thanks to the staff of the Denver Botanic Gardens in Denver, Colorado: We are particularly grateful to Solange Gignac of the Helen Fowler Library; also to Judy Elliott, Joan Franson, Joann Narverud, Andrew Pierce, Rob Proctor, Joseph V. Tomocik, and Dr. Helen Zeiner, for their help with plant identification and research. We also thank these Denver landscape architects: Jeffrey Frank, for his fine photographs of trees and shrubs, and Diane Ipsen and Alan Rollinger for their assistance with plant identification. We appreciate the help of the photographer, Cary Hazlegrove, and gardener, Ted Godfrey, who were most informative about Nantucket gardens and plant life, and past and present members of the COUNTRY LIVING staff: Maura Fidler, Louise Fiore, Theo Hewko, Robin Long Mayer, Bo Niles, Brenda Scott, and Nancy Wallin, who provided invaluable help with research and preparation.

Thanks, too, go to the individuals whose gardens are featured in the book, and who inspired and advised us: Diane and Larry Currey; Lisbeth and John Farmar-Bowers; Barbara and Marc Horovitz; Sheila and Sam Jewell; Anne and Robert Jones; Carol and Jack Kelly; Sharon Lovejoy and Jeff Prostovich; Keith Scott Morton; and Ann Voyles. We thank artists Barb Fisher and Laura Chappell. In addition, we acknowledge the other gardeners, not mentioned by name, whose ideas and artistry have helped plant the seeds of future gardens in the minds of all who read this book.

Niña Williams and Rebecca Sawyer

Index